CBC

EXPOSED

BY BRIAN LILLEY

FRE3DOM PRESS
CANADA INC.

Freedom Press
12-111 Fourth Ave., Suite 185
St. Catharines, ON L2S 3P5
Printed in the United States of America

CBC Exposed
Brian Lilley
ISBN: 978-0-9881691-0-4

FREEDOM
PRESS
CANADA INC.

We want to acknowledge www.cbcExposed.com
as the leading web authority
on the abuses of the CBC
and subsequent waste of taxpayer money.

Contents

Forword

We live in what has long been called the 500 channel universe. And Canadians have more options for watching Canadian programming than they have ever had before. We can watch sports on TSN, home and gardening shows on W Network, kids can watch cartoons all day on Treehouse and of course you can get your fill of news and opinion at Sun News Network.

Yet despite all the channel choices Canadians have, and the explosion of homegrown content, we still have CBC as a state funded broadcaster.

Why?

In the book you are holding Brian Lilley lays out the argument for why CBC should be sold off and taken off the taxpayer dole.

Few people have been as determined to get to the truth of how CBC spends your tax dollars than my Sun News colleague Brian Lilley. He has written dozens of articles for Sun Media newspapers and exposed their waste and arrogance during his Sun News program Byline.

Have you ever heard about the millions the CBC spent defending the indefensible after ruining a good doctor's name? Did you know that CBC has spent millions upon millions of dollars defending lawsuits that could have been settled with a simple apology?

And what about CBC's biases?

We all know that the state broadcaster hates conservatives but what about their handling of stories about gun owners, Israel or their vendetta against Brian and myself for exposing their spendthrift ways?

This book makes the case that the only way to rein in CBC is to sell it off and put it under the control of the private sector.

For the sake of Canada, you need to buy this book, learn its arguments and share the warning -- and the solutions it offers -- with your friends.

Ezra Levant

Prologue

I f CBC didn't exist would we invent it?

It is a question worth asking, and how you answer it might be a telltale sign as to whether you think we need a state broadcaster at all. There are literally hundreds of television channels to choose from today and more radio formats than we've ever had.

Most Canadians subscribe to cable or satellite television services that offer them everything from all-news to all-sport channels, gardening channels, family friendly channels, networks for women only and networks aimed at the basest of male instincts.

On radio, which is available freely, we have top 40 stations, classic rock, country, alternative, talk radio and more. That doesn't even include the even more specialized stations that are available on the internet or through satellite radio.

So with all that, it must be asked again, if CBC didn't exist, would we invent it?

For all the rhetoric that CBC lovers would surely offer up if asked that question, the reality is that for most Canadians the answer would be no.

CBC didn't launch broadcasting in Canada. In fact, when CBC was launched in 1936, private radio had been around for 16 years already. There were coast-to-coast broadcasts of hockey games, political events and news.

Yet remarkably someone convinced Conservative Prime Minister R.B. Bennett to launch the state broadcaster using an annual public subsidy. The words of thanks at the launch may have been the last kind words CBC ever uttered towards a conservative minded Canadian.

Today CBC burns through $100-million-tax-dollars every 30 days. That's just the taxpayer subsidy portion of their budget and doesn't include advertising revenue or the many other pots of money they dip into from mandated CRTC payments from your cable bill to other government funding programs.

In 2012 the CBC's annual subsidy from Parliament was $1.1-billion and, despite claims that their budget has been slashed, CBC is expanding all over the place including in areas that compete with the private sector such as music services, movies, and sports and, as you will see, even pornography.

Why?

Because CBC doesn't mind spending money, especially your money.

This book tells the tale of CBC's waste, but also of the victims they have left in their wake over the years. Backed by a never empty barrel of taxpayer gold, CBC has smeared many good Canadians knowing that they could likely bury most people in legal costs if a lawsuit was ever launched.

Some people, like the ones you will meet in this book, fought back and won – and you can too.

This book will help you see why CBC needs to be brought under control before they ruin more lives. The best way to discipline CBC is to sell it off. A CBC under private ownership would be unable to waste taxpayer money to run down people they disagree with.

It's time to sell the CBC.

1

Ruining The Good Doctor's Name

"I have reached the conclusion that this broadcast was indeed devastatingly defamatory of the plaintiff."

Those are the words Justice Douglas Cunningham wrote in his scathing decision on April 20, 2000. Justice Cunningham's decision was aimed squarely at CBC and its flagship investigative program, *the fifth estate.*

That decision not only marked the largest media libel award in Canadian history, it marked the end of a long and arduous process for a doctor and family man who had seen his life ripped apart by CBC's reckless journalism.

In January of 1996, Dr. Frans Leenen was a respected cardiologist, a pharmacologist and the Director of the

Hypertension Unit at the Ottawa Heart Institute. Dr. Leenen was a world recognized expert in the field of hypertension.

And then the CBC came calling.

In the first days of 1996 Paul Webster, a researcher working for *the fifth estate*, contacted Leenen to request an interview for a documentary that was in the early stages. Told that the subject was a type of drug that Leenen had extensive experience with, calcium channel blockers, the doctor agreed.

Little did he know he was being set up?

The plan to focus on Dr. Leenen and Canada's drug regulatory system was driven by a journalist and researcher from Montreal, Nicholas Regush. Regush had worked covering medical stories for the *Montreal Gazette* and *ABC News* in New York.

But Regush wasn't a neutral observer; he was in fact a long standing critic of the Health Protection Branch (HPB), then in charge of Canada's drug approval system. When controversy erupted over the use of the drug Nifedipine, a popular CCB used for hypertension and angina, it allowed Regush and an insider at the Health Protection Branch, Dr. Michelle Brill-Edwards, to tag team the drug approval system and those that worked with it.

Dr. Brill-Edwards already had an axe to grind having complained about the workings of the system to no avail. Justice Cunningham noted the fact that neither Regush nor Dr. Brill-Edwards began their project with an open mind.

"Without question, it was a sad day for all concerned when these two people united to give vent to their long-standing biases towards the Health Protection Branch of Health Canada," Cunningham wrote in his decision.

Dr. Leenen participated in the interview giving his thoughts on the use of Nifedipine. The drug had been in use in Canada since the early 1980s in a short-acting formula. A long-acting formula came on the market in the early 1990s. Yet in March 1995, a study out of the University of Washington called into question whether the short-acting version of the drug did more harm than good.

The views given by Dr. Leenen on using Nifedipine were similar to those of other doctors around the world and even of those interviewed for the program, yet in attempting to set-up a good guy vs. bad guy scenario, CBC had already decided that Leenen was the bad guy.

Using selective editing, strategically placed music and the "famous sneering feeling" that host Trish Wood gave to her questions, Dr. Frans Leenen, a respected researcher and physician, was portrayed as "a devious, dishonest, bumbling fool in order to advance a story line." Said the judge [i]

Leenen was out of the country when the show aired. He was speaking at an international conference as part of Pfizer's advisory board. CBC dismissively described this trip as a "cruise down the Nile" and insinuated that it was a kickback from the drug company for pushing their product rather than what it truly was, a gathering of doctors to discuss how best to care for patients using pharmaceuticals.

While Leenen missed the original broadcast, one of his colleagues, Dr. Myers did not.

Like Leenen, Myers had been targeted as a "bad guy" by CBC, his reputation and impartiality called into question.

The first Leenen heard about the direction the show had taken was when a colleague informed him while he was still in Egypt that CBC presented anything but a balanced view and that he himself did not come across well. He would not get to see the program until he arrived back home, and what he saw left him devastated.

Leenen said the feeling was similar to when his sister, to whom he was close, had died in a car accident.

"That's the way I felt," Leenen told The *Globe and Mail* in 2001.

"I felt that something very dear had been taken away from me. I was gone. I was like in a black hole. It was a disaster for me. Like a nightmare. That your reputation, your integrity that is so crucial for a scientist, is suddenly gone." ii

"This program said I was beholden to the drug companies."iii

Shortly after returning to Canada and the fallout from the program, a patient made a shocking claim. The patient claimed that they had been prescribed Nifedipine simply so that the doctor could get a kickback and make money from the prescription.

Leenen was crushed; the trust between doctor and patient shattered all so CBC could court controversy and "edgy" journalism. Leenen had lost a patient because the patient felt their doctor was only in it for the money.

Patients and colleagues no longer felt they could trust Dr. Leenen. The CBC program had made him appear shifty and evasive but those appearances had more to do with camera tricks and editing than reality.

One of the scenes CBC included in the program was one of Dr. Leenen fumbling to read a document presented by CBC. Leenen had not been told he'd be reviewing a document and struggled to review it without his glasses. The presentation of that film combined with the addition of sinister music, made Leenen seem hesitant and nervous when confronted.

CBC had made people think a man trying his best to read without glasses was actually guilty of medical malpractice.

Their reputations in tatters, Leenen and Myers sought an apology from CBC. Both men also offered to settle for small amounts prior to their lawsuits going to court. Leenen asked for only $10,000 plus legal costs meaning a total of about $25,000 while Myers offered to settle for an apology and $25,000. Why CBC decided to fight to the bitter end, costing taxpayers millions of dollars and putting average citizens through the ringer, has never been answered by the state broadcaster. wringer

When CBC refused to settle Leenen had no option but to sue. A major media outlet had accused him of reckless disregard for the safety of patients, and of being in the pocket of drug companies and taking kickbacks. Leaving those assertions unchallenged would have told his patients and his colleagues that CBC's claims were true.

> "Once that perception is there, that can never be taken away anymore," Leenen told the court. "The trust is crucial for the patient-doctor relationship and if that trust, for whatever reason, is broken down, then one should really give up the patient-doctor relationship. And that is actually what this patient did. At that moment he said, well I can't come back to you anymore. And he didn't come back anymore."

In the end the program would cost taxpayers an estimated $5-million. The award to Leenen stood at $950,000 in general, aggravated and punitive damages. CBC was also on the hook for Leenen's legal costs, estimated at more than $1-million.

Add in the $200,000 awarded to Myers, his legal costs and CBC's rather substantial lawyer's fees, and taxpayers could have paid for a whole new drama in primetime rather than a tragedy played out in court.

"I told Frans in 1996 that this was the strongest libel suit I had ever seen," Leenen's lawyer Richard Dearden told the Canadian Medical Association Journal. "But the CBC played dirty from the start."[iv]

While Leenen was forced to mortgage his home and risk everything to restore his name, the gang at CBC just dipped into the pockets of the Canadian taxpayer.

"Any time you take on the CBC, you're David because it is Goliath. In dealing with *the fifth estate*, you're confronting an organization that takes a scorched-earth approach to defending libel actions, backed by the financial resources of Canadian taxpayers," Leenen said. [v]

Against this Goliath, Leenen was forced to drain his savings, mortgage his home and ask for help from family members. On more than one occasion Leenen thought he would lose it all.

Paul Webster, the researcher that worked on the show and originally contacted Dr. Leenen, took advantage of that anxiety during a break in the court proceedings. Webster told Leenen that "Somebody is going to lose his shirt" and later taunted Leenen by asking "How's the mortgage going?"

Justice Cunningham called those remarks callous and insensitive.

With his reputation in tatters though, fighting CBC was just a part of Dr. Leenen's battles. All through the legal proceedings, as Leenen was using legal avenues to restore his reputation, his once supportive workplace turned dark.

"There was a change in the way colleagues perceived me. It was almost as if there had been a death in the family. And in a way it was very much like there had been a [professional] death."[vi]

Colleagues who had seen the program offered sympathies, some from as far away as Europe. Yet sympathy didn't stop Leenen from facing professional sanctions.

The ethics committee of the Heart Institute began investigating Leenen and his work, his research projects were put on hold and a senior physician at the Heart Institute wrote a letter to the head of the organization repeating CBC's claims and questioning Dr. Leenen's ethics. Influential publications, including The New England Journal of Medicine and a newsletter associated with the Canadian Society for Clinical Pharmacology, also raised questions about Leenen's ethics.

Dr. Leenen had been a member of the Canadian Society for Clinical Pharmacology from 1979 through 1996, but when the newsletter published a letter from the president of the organization he felt he had no option but to resign. All of these attacks on Leenen's integrity caused a strain on his family. At trial, his wife Mindy testified that the effect of the CBC program was to kill off one of her husband's loves.

"Before we got married Frans told me that he had two loves and asked me if I would be able to live with that.

One love was me, the other was his research. I know how deeply hurt he was and how this has destroyed one of his loves."[vii]

Mindy Leenen described watching her husband's health deteriorate. He lost weight, had trouble sleeping and experienced high levels of stress. Eventually Dr. Leenen contracted pneumonia.

The couple's social life was affected as well.

Friends and neighbours that were once close became distant and avoided the Leenens, some going so far as to change their route to avoid the couple as they walked their dog. Mindy Leenen described being shunned by the other parents when picking up her children from school.

In short, CBC destroyed the life the Leenens had known.

When the case went to trial the evidence overwhelmingly showed that CBC left out key information, distorted the views offered up by Dr. Leenen and had generally worked at making the interviews fit the story they had decided on before the project even began.

The court also had access to outtakes from the filming process.

"We have set up the idea that this committee is tainted with these kind of company-bought people." host Trish Wood is heard saying to producer Nicholas Regush.[viii]

At another point Regush encourages Wood to use her famous sneer.

The evidence taken together resulted in condemnation from the bench through a strongly worded judgment from Justice Cunningham.

> "This program failed to present a fair portrayal of Dr. Leenen and, in fact, characterized his views

dishonestly and misrepresented his long held views on many important subjects. In order to portray him in the role of "bad guy" and in order to disparage his views, the CBC took an eminent research scientist, whom they knew to be a person of high integrity and reputation, and presented him as a devious, dishonest, bumbling fool in order to advance a story line. The defendants' suggestion that the public interest was somehow being served is nonsensical. This "important story" involving the deaths of tens of thousands of patients, of tainted files within the bureaucracy, of the influence of drug manufacturers upon the regulatory process was not even important enough to make the CBC evening news. Although the program itself was re-broadcast on CBC's *Newsworld*, the only other media outlet to pick up on the story was the *Montreal Gazette*, for whom Mr. Regush had previously worked as a medical writer. This wasn't an important story at all. This was sensational journalism of the worst sort and should serve as an embarrassment to this so-called 'flagship' investigative program."
· Justice Cunninghamn[ix]

Much was made during the broadcast of Dr. Leenen's relationship with Pfizer – the significant innuendo being that he was more beholden to the company than to patient safety. As noted above, they even used against him the out-of-country conference he was attending at the time the show aired. What the viewer was never told, of course, was that Dr. Leenen was not simply going on a "cruise down the Nile", but rather was attending a working conference in Egypt as a member of Pfizer's advisory board. Broadcasting this information, however, would have weakened the defendants' portrayal of the plaintiff as one of the "bad guys".

That judgment against CBC, handed down on April 20, 2000, also came with the largest penalty ever imposed on any Canadian media company – $950,000 plus costs. CBC could have settled for 1% of that penalty and paid substantially lower legal costs if they had only been willing to say they were sorry back in 1996.

They weren't ready to say sorry in 1996, and they still weren't ready in 2000.

Rather than accept the judgment, issue an apology, pay the penalty and move on, CBC doubled down. Dipping into the wallet of the taxpayer one more time, the state broadcaster sought leave to appeal to the Supreme Court. The move would mean CBC would incur more legal costs but so would Leenen who had to pay his own way while, as a taxpayer, also funding the colossal beast that was dragging him through one more round of legal woes.

Just shy of two years later, the Supreme Court announced that they would not hear CBC's appeal and as is their custom when letting lower court rulings stand, they did not give their reasons. In essence their silence was their way of saying that Justice Cunningham's decision was the right one.

Even the silent approval of the Supreme Court though was not enough to humble CBC; the state broadcaster was unrepentant and unapologetic.

"We are disappointed with this news because we felt that these cases raised crucial questions about freedom of expression, the law of defamation, and the media's ability to report on issues of public interest," CBC said in a statement in February of 2002.

An internal note to CBC journalists by Harold Redekopp, the then head of CBC's English services, pretty much told reporters to keep to that message.

"In our view, the program raised legitimate questions based on facts," he said. "It did not conclude there was wrongdoing by Drs. Leenen and Myers."

Guy Fournier, a one-time chairman of CBC's board of directors, isn't surprised that there are so many cases where the state broadcaster fought on only to lose, rather than offering a simple apology.

"It's not the tradition of the CBC," Fournier said. "The CBC never excuses itself and never apologizes."

He also revealed that management, and not the board, decides when to fight to the bitter end and when to settle.

"For instance, when I was on the board, we asked two or three times whether it was wise to go with a lawsuit and every time we were told it is not the business of the board," Fournier said.

Leenen remarked on CBC's decision to fight this battle to the bitter end and the fact that average citizens face an uphill battle when they fight the state broadcaster with it's never ending access to taxpayer's dollars to fight legal challenges.

"Launching a libel action of this sort against the CBC involves enormous financial risk requiring monetary resources beyond the reach of most Canadians," Leenen said after the Supreme Court denied CBC's attempt to overturn Justice Cunningham's ruling.

"Even as an established professional, I could not have done it without the financial and moral support of my wife Mindy and her family. I risked personal bankruptcy to clear my name. By defending the indefensible all the way to the Supreme Court of Canada, the CBC creates libel chill for most Canadians, and not the media."

As you will see throughout this book, Frans Leenen wasn't the first victim of CBC's arrogance – and he wasn't the last. If a respected doctor helping to improve the lives of heart patients can have his reputation ruined by CBC, his life stolen away, then it can happen to you.

Was anyone ever fired?

David Studer, executive producer of the smear job on Dr. Frans Leenen never lost his job. In fact Studer has been involved with other controversial productions before and since, including the attack on fashion mogul Peter Nygard and the 15 years of stalking Brian Mulroney.

No one was ever fired for the brutal attack on Dr. Leenen and others, including Paul Webster. The researcher cited for making callous and insensitive remarks to Leenen during a break in the trial continues to get freelance work from CBC to this day.

2

Dr. Myers I presume

Like Dr. Frans Leenen, Dr. Martin Myers had a simple hope.

"All I wanted was an apology," Myers said.

Instead, like his fellow cardiologist Dr. Leenen, Dr. Myers was forced to put his life and practice on hold to defend his reputation. At the end of his lawsuit, CBC's refusal to offer a simple apology ended up costing taxpayers $350,000 in damages awarded to Myers, plus legal costs which, when both sides were added up could have once again reached into the millions. Could have? Do we not know if it did or not? We seem to have a lot of specific financial Info on this case.

Before The Heart of the Matter aired on CBC, Martin Myers was a cardiologist treating patients at Toronto's

Sunnybrook Hospital. Like Leenen, Myers had willingly participated in what he thought was an investigative report into the use of Nifedipine, a calcium channel blocker used to treat heart disease.

Myers sat down to watch *the fifth estate* program at 8pm on February 27, 1996. He would later call it the longest 50 minutes of his life.

In trying to establish their story, CBC had set up good guys and bad guys in the debate over how Nifedipine should be used. As a trial judge would later find, the state broadcaster unfairly put Dr. Myers down as a bad guy who didn't care if patients died. Myers was accused of killing at least one patient and investigated by the hospital he worked for, argued Justice Denise Bellamy in the court decision she issued.

"The widow of a former patient congratulated the CBC on the 'exposé of Dr. Myers' in the program. She wrote that she 'watched with horror and jubilation as the facts were revealed', as she had always felt that Dr. Myers was responsible for her husband's death and that the CBC 'exposé' only corroborated her suspicions. She then asked whether this could lead to a class action law suit. Dr. Livingstone, Vice-president of Professional Affairs at Sunnybrook Hospital, facilitated an investigation of Dr. Myers' handling of the complainant's late husband's case. Ultimately, the conduct of Dr. Myers and his staff was found to meet all standards, and the concerns were found to be groundless. The tone of the letter and the subsequent investigation confirm that the program directly affected the professional life of Dr. Myers, in addition to causing him substantial personal suffering."

Knowing that his medical career was in jeopardy, Myers sued. In his statement of claim, Myers said that CBC made several innuendos through their editing and presentation of the interviews they conducted with him:

Dr. Myers realized that Nifedipine was killing thousands of patients and did not care;
In recommending the long-acting pills of Nifedipine, Dr. Myers was dishonest;

His opinion was completely contrary to accepted medical practice and hence he did not know what he was talking about or was intentionally misleading the Canadian public;
Dr. Myers was helping Bayer push a dangerous capsule and pill which he knew to be dangerous;
He was trying to stifle valid and accurate revelations of Nifedipine's capacity to kill patients;
In his role as a member of the committee
selected by the HPB to review Nifedipine
and CCBs, he acted dishonestly.

He did not have the competence or stature to be on the committee; and He refused to be interviewed again because he was afraid the truth would be revealed that he was dishonest.

Myers never claimed that the statements he gave to the state broadcaster were false but that "the overall impression created by the words and the images is alleged to be defamatory."

The trial judge found all eight innuendos were defamatory of Dr. Myers as proven by the evidence. Although Justice Bellamy did find that the sixth claim was protected by the defence of fair comment, all the others stood.

"While the defence of fair comment provides broad protection to journalists to publish whatever they want, it also imposes a minimal standard of fairness which has not been met," Justice Bellamy wrote.

"In pursuit of a sensational story about a potentially serious drug regulation issue, *the fifth estate* took clips and excerpts of remarks made by a leading cardiologist out of their complex context and presented them in a simplified 'good-guy, bad-guy' format. ...Given all the facts they had collected and reviewed, I cannot accept that they honestly believed that the highly damaging innuendoes they were conveying were expressions of the truth about the issue," read one of the more damaging portions of Bellamy's ruling.

She went on to accuse CBC of "acting in bad faith" and said that the state broadcaster had shown "dishonesty" in their dealings with Dr. Myers. She also concluded that the defendants, all CBC employees or contractors, "were acting maliciously."

Of course CBC did not accept the ruling, and dipped into taxpayer's wallets once again to pay for an appeal that they would ultimately lose. For Dr. Martin Myers there was a real financial price to be paid in order to clear his name, Myers had to shut down his practice for 7 weeks to prepare and participate in the 5 1/2 week trial.

"Trust me, there are easier ways to make a living than by going to court," Myers told the Canadian Medical Association Journal in 2000. "I'd have done anything not to have gone through this. I told the CBC right from the beginning that all I wanted was an apology and they said No. It was as if they were saying they could not be wrong."

3

CBC Shows Its Hatred For Success

Peter Nygard's story is the kind CBC would normally celebrate – one of an immigrant who moved as a child from Helsinki, Finland to the small town of Deloraine, Manitoba, but went on to make it big on the world stage.

But CBC doesn't like Peter Nygard.

In a 2010 documentary about the fashion mogul, CBC used testimony from people who are described by police as "serial fraudsters" to portray Peter Nygard as a man whose personal life is filled with nothing but partying and sex. The documentary was supposed to be about Nygard as a boss, but instead focused almost exclusively on his personal life, and painted a very dark and unfair picture.

Nygard came to Canada from Finland with his parents and younger sister in 1952 when he was just ten years old. The family settled in Deloraine, a town about a four hour drive from Winnipeg. Having arrived with only what they could carry, the family's start in Canada was modest to say the least. Their first home was a converted coal shack.

"We had no running water, didn't have heat; we lit up a stove in the middle of the room," Nygard said in a video biography posted on his website.

That first family home measured just 15 feet by 13 feet, and the stove in the middle of the room used to heat the place was also used for cooking.

Nygard described the use of a rusty barrel to melt snow for water and the need to use an outdoor toilet at 40 below zero temperatures. He related how he, his parents and his younger sister all slept in the same bed at times, a bed that sagged in the middle. To help pay for groceries he and his sister would collect empty bottles from wherever they could find them and return them to local stores for the meagre deposit refund.

From those humble beginnings, Nygard went on to build one of the most successful women's fashion houses in the world. Nygard's fashion designs are carried by top department stores such as The Bay, Sears and Dillard's as well as his own chain of 200 branded stores worldwide. The company employs 12,000 people globally with operations in Canada, the US, Hong Kong, the Middle East, South Africa, Kenya, Egypt, India, Bangladesh, Indonesia and Cambodia.

This success has allowed Nygard to donate millions of dollars to charity with a special emphasis on breast cancer. His company lists breast cancer as its main charity of choice and has organized gala events, runs for the cure and more. Nygard even donated money to help with the Manitoba Breast Tumour Bank, an organization that helps researchers better understand the disease as they look for a cure.

Perhaps it was his level of success that prompted CBC to target Nygard with a one-hour special program on *the fifth estate* in April 2010.

CBC interviewed a small number of former employees who described him as a tough boss, prone to yelling, some even saying he crossed the line into abuse. The names and contact information for these people were provided to CBC by a disgruntled former human resource manager who made sure to select only those employees who were known to hold a personal grudge against Nygård.

It would hardly be surprising that a self-made multi-millionaire might be a tough boss. Taking an initial investment of just a few thousand dollars in 1967 and turning it into a company with global reach and sales in the hundreds of millions isn't easy to do, some egos might get bruised along the way.

In their attempt to smear Nygard as an awful man to work for, CBC's documentary focused on his private life and specifically his luxurious home at Nygard Cay in the Bahamas. For the most outrageous allegations, CBC relied on statements made by a pair of fraud artists, Allan and Michelle May.

The Mays worked for Nygard during the months of July and August 2003. That's it. They left their employment on bad terms, and admitted that they stole documents from Nygard when they left. The Mays are described by police in St. Lucia as "serial fraudsters" who have bilked investors and others over the years. Despite this track record, CBC relied heavily on Allan and Michelle May, as they attempted to smear Nygard as not only a bad employer, but also as a sexual predator.

In their broadcast, CBC allowed the Mays to insinuate that Peter Nygard had acted inappropriately with a 16-year-old girl. The couple provided no proof to the CBC. The broadcaster was aware of the bad reputation the couple had but built the smear around their statements anyway. Before airing the program CBC was provided a notarized statement from the young woman in question disputing the statements made by the Mays, including the fact that she was 18 not 16-years-old. Court documents also state that CBC operatives even tracked down the girl prior to the broadcast of the program, but declined to interview her.

Lawyers for Nygard also provided CBC with evidence given by the Mays under oath in an American court case. In that case, heard before an American federal court, the Mays admitted to lies and other dishonest, and sometimes criminal, conduct. None of this swayed CBC from going ahead with their program which relied heavily on testimony from a pair of shady characters and claims they made about a woman to whom CBC had never even spoken.

To Peter Nygard it was clear that he was now under full attack from Canada's state broadcaster.

"It is so tragic to have an institution like this just attack you," Nygard said. "I never figured in a million years that it could even happen... that they would so recklessly go after an individual."

"It sort of shatters your whole dream of this country."

According to Nygard, CBC used Allan and Michelle May to smear him and he says the state broadcaster was also involved in a criminal conspiracy with his Bahamian neighbour and enemy – hedge fund billionaire Louis Bacon. Nygard states in his own deposition before the courts that the goal of that conspiracy, which has Bacon at the centre of it, is to oust him from his lavish home in the Bahamas. Nygard's claims have not been proven in court at this point.

Nygard Cay is situated at the Western tip of the exclusive community known as Lyford Cay on New Providence, Bahamas. Started in 1954 by Canadian brewing magnate and industrialist E.P. Taylor, Lyford Cay has been a second or first home, to the likes of Sean Connery, Henry Ford II, Aga Khan, Shania Twain as well as many other well-to-do people from Canada, Britain and the United States. It is a gated community with its own security and property owners association.

In 1987, Peter Nygard began building what he describes as his Mayan temple of an estate, one he is only too happy to share with others. Louis Bacon purchased the adjoining property, known as Point House, several years later. At first the two men got along, but eventually that changed.

In 2004, a dispute broke out between Nygard and Bacon over an access road leading to Nygard Cay. The access road went through Bacon's property but was considered an easement meaning Nygard and his guests had every legal right to use the road. Bacon, though, was uncomfortable with Nygard's parties, his lifestyle and his practice of inviting locals to join in the festivities at the palatial resort.

According to court documents filed by Nygard, Bacon conspired with the Lyford Cay Property Owners Association and its manager Mary Braithwaite to discredit Nygard and try to force him out. Eventually

CBC was contacted by people associated with Bacon and salacious tales were told. Nygard claims that Bacon and his associates worked with CBC to produce the documentary called *"Larger than Life."*

Along the way Nygard says, CBC threw ethics and responsibility out the window.

"There is overwhelming evidence," Nygard wrote in documents filed with the court, "that Bacon contacted employees of the Canadian Broadcasting Corporation ('CBC') who were planning a scandalous documentary about me for broadcast on a program called *the fifth estate.* He promised to provide them with material for a story that would take me down."

One of the people hired to help CBC set up their documentary was Jerry Forrester. Forrester is an ex-FBI agent who claims he kidnapped people and transported them to the Bahamas without court orders during his time on the US government payroll.

CBC hired him for a fee of $1,500 per day plus expenses to help set up interviews with people willing to talk about Peter Nygard. One of the interviews he set up was between CBC's producers and "serial fraudsters" Allan and Michelle May.

It was the Mays who would appear on camera insinuating that Nygard had been sexually aggressive and inappropriate with women but Forrester, according to court documents, was willing to pay women to make up such claims.

After CBC aired their "documentary" smearing Nygard, the fashion mogul hired former Scotland Yard Detective Inspector Alick Morrison. Morrison was given the task of figuring out how that show came together, and to follow-up on Nygard's hunch that CBC was used as part of a conspiracy by Nygard's neighbours.

Morrison, a British national, who retired after more than 30 years with Scotland Yard, had recently been employed as a mentor to the head of the serious crime unit in Basra, Iraq, and to the head of the counter narcotics police unit in Helmand province, Afghanistan. Morrison's job now was to find out who was behind the scam to discredit Nygard and harm his reputation.

Posing as an agent from a European fashion house that also wanted to discredit Nygard, Morrison was able to meet CBC's PI Jerry Forrester in Miami.

His first meeting with Forrester in July 2010, just three months after the documentary aired, didn't allay any suspicions that a conspiracy was afoot.

Forrester bragged about being a security consultant to the Lyford Cay Property Owners Association and a friend and golf partner to some of the wealthiest people in the world. During their meetings Forrester also told Morrison about being close friends with Steve Davis, a private investigator on the payroll of Nygard nemesis Louis Bacon. Davis is also at times referred to as Bacon's head of security.

According to Morrison's sworn affidavit, filed in Bahamian court, Forrester described Peter Nygard as a "dirt bag" and someone that the LCPOA and Louis Bacon were intent on driving out of Lyford Cay.

All of this should be troubling, considering Forrester's role in helping CBC construct their story about Nygard. But, according to Morrison, even with several warning signals, CBC kept on paying Forrester $1,500 a day to help *the fifth estate.*

Forrester told Morrison that he approached CBC producer Tim Sawa and offered to work with a friend to find local girls willing to "say anything disparaging" about Peter Nygard provided they were paid a fee. Sawa declined to pay interview suspects but decided to keep paying Forrester just the same.

Morrison saw this as a tacit endorsement of Forrester's methods by CBC.

"Even after Forrester offered to bribe or pay witnesses, the producer of the CBC programme, Tim Sawa, continued to use him without sanction, thereby condoning his actions or turning a blind eye to his methods," Morrison wrote in his testimony.

Jerry Forrester was a man who claimed to have kidnapped people while he was working with the FBI; claimed to have transported a man back to the Bahamas who later died in police custody; and he had offered to find "witnesses" to speak out against Nygard if they were paid, yet CBC kept him on, paying him on behalf of the Canadian taxpayer.

Forrester helped CBC connect with Allan and Michelle May, who had left their jobs in Nygard Cay in August of 2003, after just six weeks of employment there. Just around the time CBC was interviewing the Mays, the pair was found guilty of civil fraud for failing to pay back $189,000 they bilked from investors.

Police in St. Lucia told the *Winnipeg Sun* that the couple has "a history of committing frauds in other Caribbean islands, leaving each jurisdiction for the next island when identified by law enforcement officials."

A spokesman for Nygard international told the *Sun* that the arrest was further proof that CBC based their story on faulty evidence. "Nygard's lawyers had provided the CBC pages of facts on the past fraudulent conduct of the Mays. In spite of this, CBC's *fifth estate* chose to base

50% of their tabloid-style story on false testimony from the Mays," the spokesman said.

Forrester had set up CBC with the Mays and had offered to find girls willing to fabricate stories about Nygard but according to Morrison's sworn affidavit, there was one woman in particular whom the CBC didn't want Forrester talking to – the young woman with the most outrageous allegation made against Peter Nygard.

During one of their chats, many of which are on tape, Forrester told Morrison that CBC paid him $9,000 to track down a previously unidentified woman who had stayed at Nygard's resort in 2003. This was the same girl that Allan and Michelle May had claimed came to them fearful for her safety. The woman, named Maribel Rodriguez, was tracked down by Forrester in the Dominican Republic just one day before CBC was slated to air the documentary.

"They [Forrester and friends] made a phone call to CBC to see if they wanted her vehicle stopped and Maribel to be interviewed," Morrison wrote in his affidavit. "CBC told them not to stop the vehicle and to conclude the surveillance."

Had CBC stopped the car they would have discovered their story was full of holes and they would either have had to scrap the broadcast or seriously rewrite the story.

They chose to plough ahead with their smear job.

CBC admitted on air that they received a sworn statement from Maribel Rodriguez, through Nygard's lawyers, prior to the documentary airing. The statement said that she was an adult at the time she visited Nygard Cay and that nothing untoward had happened during her visit. "During my stay at NCBR, in 2003, my stay was pleasant and fun," the statement from Rodriguez reads. "I enjoyed interacting with all the people there. The men were real gentlemen, including Mr. Nygard; and the women and Models were all friendly."

That statement was just one of many supportive statements given to CBC ahead of the broadcast. For most media organizations who cannot rely on an endless supply of taxpayer's dollars to pay for lawsuits, these statements combined with a lack of evidence of actual wrongdoing by Nygard, might have been enough to stop the program from airing. At the least it would have put the broadcast on hold until facts could be checked and re-checked. Not at CBC, though.

Instead they went ahead with a program that used the testimony of disgruntled employees complaining about their old boss. The program served no public interest beyond passing gossip off as fact, and smearing the name of a man who has created 12,000 jobs where none existed, funded millions of dollars in charitable causes and did it all in the face of extremely humble beginnings.

"It amazes me that an institution like this is able to do all those questionable and destructive things – an institution that is funded by the taxpayer to $1.2-billion per year – and with that, they can then go ahead and attack their own citizens in a reckless and an unfair manner," Nygard said.

Of course Nygard hasn't taken any of this lying down. He's launched civil and criminal proceedings in Canada and the Bahamas to fight back. Unlike some victims, such as Dr. Frans Leenen, Nygard has the ability to do this. Nevertheless, this could be the fight of his life!

Scotland Yard veteran Alick Morrison believes there is ample evidence of a conspiracy against Nygard that includes Louis Bacon, Mary Braithwaite the manager of Lyford Cay Property Owners Association, Jerry Forrester and others. One of the others is Pericles Maillis, the Bahamian lawyer for both Bacon and the LCPOA.

"Pericles Maillis is recorded offering to pay $10,000 to a girl to make a false allegation of serious sexual abuse," Morrison wrote in his statement to the court. "He was in conversation with Jerry Forrester."

As Nygard fights to clear his name in court, presenting what Morrison calls "significant evidence" of a campaign to defame the fashion mogul, sources close to the company say they are worried CBC is planning a second installment of their hatchet job. This concern is supported by statements filed in Bahamian court proceedings which reveal that there are continuing attempts to obtain false evidence from women about Nygard's conduct for use in a CBC broadcast.

Despite all his money, his success and generosity, Peter Nygard, was another victim of the CBC smear machine. If they can do this to a man as powerful as Peter Nygard, what could they do to you?

4

The Attempted Take Down
Of A Former Prime Minister

It was the lowest moment of his life.

That's how CBC journalist Harvey Cashore described the day that former Prime Minister Brian Mulroney had just been awarded $2.1-million in a lawsuit against the federal government.

Cashore was convinced that Mulroney was guilty of taking kickbacks related to Air Canada's 1988 decision to buy a fleet of Airbus A320 jets, but here was a federal court awarding the massive payout in a libel settlement. The CBC journalist told reporters years later that he "told his boss he wanted to drop the subject."[x]

But, feeling that if he dropped the story he had staked his career on, he wouldn't be able to face his two young sons, Cashore pushed ahead. Despite pursuing the story for 15 years, he would ultimately fail in proving, or having a judicial inquiry prove, that Brian Mulroney was guilty of anything more than bad judgment when it came to the company he kept.

"I spent 15 years, imagine being me, I spent 15 years with one question, where'd the money go, and we didn't find out," Cashore told *The Hill Times* just days before the Oliphant Commission reported its findings into the dealings between Mulroney and German-Canadian businessman Karlheinz Schreiber.[xi]

Cashore wasn't sure, at the end of a decade and a half, if the process was worth it.

"There are untold millions spent by Canadian taxpayers on this story, whether it's in court costs, or RCMP investigations or the Oliphant Commission, untold millions," Cashore said.

What he didn't include in the tally of the untold millions was the cost to taxpayers of CBC spending 15 years attempting to run a parallel prosecution of a politician for whom those inside the state broadcaster had never hidden their disdain.

Starting in 1995, CBC's *fifth estate* would produce nine documentaries on the Airbus Affair, all attempting but never succeeding, to link Mulroney to illegal kickbacks.

The public attempt to link Mulroney with illegal secret payments had begun in 1994 with the publication of *On The Take,* Stevie Cameron's account of the Mulroney years in power. It was a book filled with explosive allegations but a book that even former CBC journalist Alex Roslin called "a tad partisan."[xii]

Cameron, a former host with CBC's *fifth estate* and a writer with The *Globe and Mail*, didn't link Mulroney to Airbus commission kickbacks directly in *On the Take*. That book painted a picture of a government with a "reputation for sleaze," running on "flagrant kickbacks."

Over the coming years Cameron, Cashore and the state broadcaster would take run after run at Mulroney trying to prove he was guilty.

They never succeeded.

CBC began investigating claims that Air Canada's 1988 purchase of Airbus jets involved kickbacks in the fall of 1994 just after Cameron's book was published. The initial *fifth estate* program aired on March 28, 1995, focusing on Karlheinz Schreiber and Frank Moores, a former premier of Newfoundland and, at one time, the most powerful lobbyist in Ottawa.

Working with accountant and long-time Schreiber associate Giorgio Pelossi, CBC painted a picture of Schreiber as a man bribing his way across the Canadian political landscape and Moores, the former premier and close friend of Brian Mulroney, his willing accomplice.

Pelossi had worked with Schreiber since the late 1960s, including helping set up companies in a way that kept money hidden from the tax man. In the early 1990s however the two had a falling out over money, filed competing lawsuits and learned to despise each other.

Pelossi had spent time in Swiss, Italian and American prisons, yet to CBC, Stevie Cameron and the RCMP, he was always a reliable witness.[xiii] It was the same pattern they would later follow in covering fashion mogul Peter Nygard, using people with less than stellar reputations to make wild accusations.

It was Pelossi's expertise that was crucial to the claims made in that initial CBC broadcast.

By the summer of 1995, the RCMP was briefing their new Liberal political masters in Ottawa that the former Progressive Conservative Prime Minister, Brian Mulroney was under investigation for taking millions in kickbacks from the Airbus purchase - much of the impetus for this investigation driven by reporting from CBC and Cameron.

On September 29, 1995, a letter had been sent to Swiss authorities seeking assistance in what was alleged to be a massive bribery scandal.

The Mounties claimed that Mulroney, Moores and Schreiber had squirreled away money in secret Swiss bank accounts and defrauded Canadian taxpayers of millions of dollars. Only by lifting the veil of secrecy surrounding the Swiss banking system could justice be done.

Sending the letter, a fishing expedition of sorts by prosecutors, was a huge gamble and one that had been approved of in the upper levels of the Chrétien Liberal government. The departments of Justice Minister Alan Rock and Solicitor General Herb Gray had each been

---

Around the same time the Mulroney's memoirs were released, former Liberal Prime Minister Jean Chrétien released his book, *My Years as Prime Minister*. While Mulroney was treated to an exposé from *fifth estate* filled with innuendo, Chrétien was treated with kid gloves.

Mulroney was blasted for not spilling the beans on Schreiber but surely Chrétien could have been grilled on the sponsorship scandal, the billions taken from the EI fund or Shawinigate. It was not to be.

briefed on the letter. They both signed off on the RCMP's decision to claim that a former Prime Minister was a crook – based upon the word of journalists who hated Mulroney and a convict in the form of Pelossi with an axe to grind.

The entire affair would end with the Government of Canada paying $2.1-million to Mulroney for legal and public relations expenses and the revelation that Mulroney never had a Swiss bank account.

Finding out that a former Prime Minister, one who Cashore and his CBC cohorts so obviously despise, had just been awarded a multimillion dollar court settlement may have been the lowest moment in Cashore's life, but it didn't stop him from pursuing the story.

In the years after the lawsuit was settled, CBC would produce 7 more documentaries trying to link Mulroney to illegal payments. Cashore and Cameron would work together on a book, *The Last Amigo,* putting more innuendo into the public square, and Cashore would eventually release his own book, *The Truth Shows Up.*

That last book, *The Truth Shows Up*, should have been a crowning achievement for Cashore. Instead, perhaps as a sign of how little Canadians cared about this "scandal," the book sold poorly – less than 2,000 copies – and was cited as one of the titles that pushed publisher Key Porter toward bankruptcy.[xiv]

When Brian Mulroney launched his personal memoirs in September 2007, there was a notable name missing from the 1,000 pages detailing the ups and downs of Mulroney's life – Karlheinz Schreiber. The omission infuriated Cashore and the gang at *fifth estate,* and within weeks they had sprung to action to "correct" the record.

Brian Mulroney: The Unauthorized Chapter was a classic *fifth estate* smear job. Alternating between dark music and tunes that sounded like they were lifted from a spy movie, the program pushed innuendo to new levels. There was no new evidence that Brian Mulroney was guilty of any crime, but that didn't stop CBC from attempting to have viewers believe the opposite was true.

"A former Canadian Prime Minister on a business trip to Europe makes a private side trip," host Linden MacIntyre states over music worthy of a Bond movie. MacIntyre goes on to describe Mulroney checking into a "high priced" hotel in Zurich for a meeting with Schreiber.

The episode continues by rehashing familiar ground, using the same archive footage they had used time and again while attempting to link Mulroney to Schreiber's secret commissions. All of this is interspersed with footage from a new interview with Schreiber conducted just prior to his detention and pending deportation to Germany.

While MacIntyre mentions that Schreiber is accused of bribery, fraud and tax evasion in Germany he intones that "his only crime in Canada – embarrassing the powerful."

Schreiber had been arrested in Toronto in 1999, and was subject to an extradition order, signed by Liberal Justice Minister Irwin Cotler, since 2004. Through legal manoeuvres, he had been able to stay in the country but his options were running out.

It was under these desperate circumstances that CBC gave Schreiber a platform in the fall of 2007 and replayed the story they had told so many times before. There is little new information revealed in the 42 minute production; just more claims by Schreiber that Mulroney didn't want his cash payments made public.

Schreiber is upfront with MacIntyre that he will do whatever he can to stay in Canada and avoid jail in Germany.

If it dawns on MacIntyre that perhaps Schreiber would go so far as to lead on a journalist and smear a former Prime Minister in order to remain here, he doesn't let on. Neither does he present this possibility to the viewer. Instead he dresses Schreiber up as an honest man wronged – and hung out to dry – by his rich and powerful former friends.

The episode aired on Halloween night 2007.

The next day, The House of Commons erupted with news of the $300,000 cash payments from Schreiber to Mulroney even though this information was made public in 2003.

"Mr. Speaker, new and disturbing information has come to light about a former Prime Minister of this country," Liberal Leader Stéphane Dion thundered at the opening of Question Period on November 1, 2007, the day after *the fifth estate* aired their *Unauthorized Chapter* on Mulroney's life.

"This information damages the integrity of the office of the Prime Minister, a key component of our democracy. The current Prime Minister must do everything he can to get to the bottom of this issue. Will the Prime Minister take every step necessary regarding this disturbing information about Mr. Mulroney to get to the bottom of this matter?"[xv]

A week later, with CBC leading the daily charge to connect Mulroney to shady or even illegal payments and kickbacks, Schreiber files an affidavit in a Toronto court, claiming he sealed a deal with Mulroney to have the former PM become his lobbyist two days before he left office.

The affidavit contradicted previous statements that Schreiber had given under oath. Eventually he would admit under cross examination that parts of his court filing were false – but that affidavit helped him obtain a short term victory: he was allowed to stay in Canada once the government agreed to call a public inquiry.

All of this was driven by *the fifth estate's* reporting, and the relentless repetition on CBC radio and television.

CBC and *the fifth estate* rushed out a new and updated version of their Halloween episode and aired it just three weeks later, after the inquiry was called.

The Inquiry

The RCMP had investigated the so-called Airbus Affair for ten years. They had initially advised newly minted Liberal Justice Minister Allan Rock, back in December 1993, that there were no grounds for an investigation. All that changed when Stevie Cameron and CBC started pushing through the story, pushing their vendettas against Mulroney.

Yet even with all of this, the RCMP had closed the file on Airbus in 2003, stating publicly that they could find no evidence of wrongdoing.

This wasn't good enough for the gang at CBC and especially *the fifth estate.*

The inquiry and the preceding Parliamentary committee investigation had been prompted by *the fifth estate* report of October 31, and the front page story of

Toronto's *Globe and Mail* newspaper on that same day. CBC and The *Globe* had worked together on a story about Mulroney not paying taxes on his $300,000 payments at the time he received the money.

"Brian Mulroney: the payments and the taxman," read *The Globe* headline above a photo of Mulroney and Schreiber together during Mulroney's days in office.

The fact that Mulroney had taken the cash payments had been revealed in *The Globe* four years earlier by author and lawyer William Kaplan. What was new was the information that Mulroney did not immediately pay taxes on the money, but did so several years later, through what is called a "voluntary disclosure."

The opposition Liberals who had authorized the $2.1-million payment to Mulroney for what had appeared to be a political witch hunt now wanted the payment back.

"Why is the Conservative government now afraid of such a public inquiry? Liberal MP Robert Thibault thundered in the House of Commons.

There was little new information and what was new showed Mulroney paying taxes. For the time being, the government stonewalled the idea of an inquiry. This mess was from a different era, from a different political party than the new Conservatives now led by Stephen Harper. There was little upside for Harper in getting involved in the controversy.

Then two things happened that really left Harper with no option.

First, Schreiber filed that affidavit claiming he hired Mulroney before the latter left office as Prime Minister. Schreiber also began telling reporters that he had written a letter to Prime Minister Harper in April 2007 informing him of this. Each time Schreiber spoke to reporters he hinted that he had more to tell, and would reveal all in a public inquiry.

Harper had initially declared the dealings between Mulroney and Schreiber as "private business," and rejected the idea of calling an inquiry. His office stated publicly that he had never seen the letter, a claim later backed up when it was revealed that officials working in the correspondence office had not considered it important enough to share with the Prime Minister.

After nearly two weeks of media fever, driven in large part by the CBC's fixation on Schreiber, Mulroney himself called for a public inquiry. Stephen Harper appointed University of Waterloo president David Johnston to examine the issue and draw up terms of reference.

Johnston would eventually recommend a limited public inquiry, saying that there was no need for a wide ranging inquiry that would reopen the entire Airbus Affair which had been thoroughly investigated by the RCMP.

Before the inquiry, headed up by Manitoba judge Jeffrey Oliphant, could begin, Members of Parliament launched their own inquiry using a House of Commons committee as the venue.

Under questioning at committee, Schreiber laughed when asked by Bloc MP Carolle Lavallée whether Mulroney was involved in Airbus and had received payments.

"I received great laughs when the story came out that Brian Mulroney was involved with Airbus," Schreiber said. Schreiber told the committee that, in those days, Air Canada was definitely a Liberal organization and didn't want much to do with Mulroney's Conservatives. He told Lavallée that had Mulroney shown up within five miles of Air Canada headquarters, suggesting a course of action, the executives at the government owned airline would have done the exact opposite.

At his committee appearance on December 13, 2007, Mulroney was definitive in his statements.

"First, I never received a cent from anyone for services rendered to anyone in connection with the purchase by Air Canada from Airbus of 34 aircraft in 1988.

"Second, I did not receive a cent from Thyssen Industries or any other client of Mr. Schreiber while I was in office.

"Third, I have never had a lawyer in Geneva, or elsewhere in Switzerland, except to defend myself against the false charges laid against me in 1995.

"Fourth, I have never had a bank account in Switzerland.

"Fifth, neither I nor anyone on my behalf, ever asked Mr. Schreiber or his lawyer to perjure themselves or otherwise lie about the payments received from him."[xvi]

Cashore, the lead investigator and producer for CBC's coverage of Mulroney was utterly dismissive of the former Prime Minister's statements.

"While there's no evidence to disprove what Mr. Mulroney is saying, we couldn't find any evidence so far to corroborate it," Cashore said.[xvii]

In the spring of 2009, the Oliphant Inquiry got underway. A large portion of Ottawa's former city hall was taken over for the hearings and the media coverage of them.

To ensure impartiality, the inquiry reached far outside the usual Ottawa, Toronto, Montreal triangle, all cities in which Brian Mulroney had done extensive business. Justice Oliphant, then Associate Chief Justice of the Court of Queen's Bench in Manitoba, was flown in to preside over the affair while Richard Wolson, also from Winnipeg, served as chief counsel for the inquiry.

Over three months of testimony was heard.

Mulroney and Schreiber both took the stand as did several other key witnesses. The reporting was breathless; the actual news coming out of the event was thin.

On May 31, 2010, the Oliphant report was released. The commission had cost Canadian taxpayers $16-million to conduct and, in the end, it told us what we all knew: Brian Mulroney had bad judgment when it came to his dealings, particularly his cash dealings with Karlheinz Schreiber.

The Oliphant report stated that the money to pay Mulroney had come from funds in a Schreiber controlled Swiss bank account, code named Britain, which in turn had been funded by another account code named Frankfurt. The source of the money for Mulroney ultimately originated with Schreiber's secret commissions from the Airbus sale but there was no evidence presented to show that Mulroney knew this or had acted inappropriately in any way while he was Prime Minister.

"I find that Mr. Schreiber was a man with whom Mr. Mulroney had met numerous times on official business, particularly over the latter years of his tenure as Prime Minister of Canada," Justice Oliphant wrote. "I find that nothing inappropriate occurred during the meetings that Mr. Schreiber had with Mr. Mulroney during Mr. Mulroney's tenure as Prime Minister."

Oliphant would declare Mulroney's cash dealings inappropriate for a former Prime Minister but, of course, not illegal.

There had been ten years of police investigations, 15 years of CBC spending millions travelling the world to run a parallel prosecution of a former Prime Minister, a series of Parliamentary hearings and finally a public inquiry. None showed that Mulroney had taken illegal kickbacks from the sale of jets to Air Canada in 1988. But this didn't matter to Cashore: just because no one had proven Mulroney was guilty didn't mean he was innocent.

Brian Mulroney is hardly a sympathetic figure to many Canadians, but one has to wonder how much of the animosity towards Canada's 18th prime minister is driven by the unrelenting attempt by the CBC to link him to illegal payments that neither they nor law enforcement could provide any evidence for.

CBC wasn't content to simply hound Brian Mulroney using the forces of *the fifth estate*, they wanted to use their entertainment budget as well.

Mulroney the Opera was a $3.7-million production commissioned by CBC and funded directly by them to the tune of $1-million. The plan was to produce an opera on Mulroney's life that would be shown in theatres first and CBC television second. Before it could even hit the silver screen, CBC dropped the project, surrendered broadcast rights and took their name off the project.

It's tough to blame them. Not only was the opera a smear job as one might expect, but it was a bad one at that. Not even a single memorable tune that could be hummed on the way out of the theatre; just a series of bad songs portraying Mulroney as an American wanna-be with no ethics and an unquenchable thirst for power.

No other prime minister has been subject to such ridicule at taxpayers' expense as Brian Mulroney.

How much money has CBC spent on this file? How many untold hours did staff and freelancers spend trying to prove what amounted to their own personal view of a politician? And why had CBC given this one particular topic a seemingly unlimited budget?

"Looking back, I think I spent too much time on it and got too concerned about it, both because I thought my reputation was being tarnished and that we needed to know where the money went," Cashore said as the Oliphant commission wrapped up. "I talk about missing a family vacation and that kind of thing, and looking back, what was more important? I think I've learned to be a little less focused on my work."[xviii]

CBC's Cashore can now spend more time with his family and focus his work elsewhere, but his 15 years spent dogging a Prime Minister and smearing his name will likely mean Mulroney will never fully recover his reputation.

5

Taking Aim At The Competition

There are two things CBC doesn't like to be questioned on. How it spends the money it extorts from Canadians and how it gets that money.

Most Canadians know that CBC is funded by the taxpayer, although polling shows that most have no idea the full extent of that funding. In addition to the more than $1.1-billion that the federal government provides through an annual subsidy, CBC is able to access millions more through a series of funding mechanisms set up by the government or government agencies.

In 2011 the Local Programming Improvement Fund provided CBC with $40-million. The CBC and its French counterpart Radio-Canada picked up more than $90-million from the Canadian Media Fund. Then there are the production credits and tax breaks that they can access by working with independent producers to make their shows rather than making the shows themselves.

Add in the CRTC's preferential treatment given to CBC specialty channels as their news network, which has mandatory carriage in every home in Canada, a prime placement on the dial and a mandatory fee that is almost 4 times what competitors are granted by the CRTC and you can add in another $100-million plus.

In 2007, Pierre Karl Peladeau dared to challenge some of that funding and found himself berated in the Quebec media as a thug set on destroying Canadian culture.

For years Canadian cable companies have been forced to hand over hundreds of millions of dollars to fund pet projects of the CRTC, Canada's broadcast regulator. Both the Local Programming Improvement Fund and the Canadian Media Fund, formerly called the Canadian Television Fund, are paid for by levies placed on Canada's cable and satellite companies, and then passed on to you as a consumer.

In order to pay for their projects the CRTC requires cable and satellite companies to fork over 5% of their revenues for the media fund and 1.5% of their revenues to pay for the local programming fund. Note that the requirement is a percentage of revenue and not profit. Essentially 6.5% of your cable bill goes to pay for these two funds.

By late 2006 and early 2007, two of Canada's cable giants who also own television stations had had enough.

Jim Shaw, then CEO of Shaw Communications a cable, satellite and broadcasting giant, wrote to the head of the Canadian Television Fund stating that he was tired of subsidizing the CBC and programs that no one watched.

"Over the past 10 years, Shaw has contributed over $350-million in direct subsidies to the Canadian production industry," Shaw wrote. His assessment of the fund wasn't pretty, saying it "has become nothing more than a means of subsidizing broadcasters, pay and specialty services and independent producers to produce Canadian television programming that few watch and has no commercial or exportable value."

Shaw stopped his monthly payments to the fund; valued at $56-million annually, saying that he wouldn't contribute another penny until changes were made. Despite his strong words and complaints that CBC took more than one-third of the fund's money without having the audience share to back it up, Shaw was not attacked by anyone at the state broadcaster.

The same could not be said when it came to Quebecor CEO Pierre Karl Peladeau.

Peladeau's Quebecor owned the dominant cable company in Quebec, Videotron. That fact made his company one of the biggest contributors to the fund.

Peladeau was also frustrated with the way the CTF was being run, including the fact that 37% of the funds were set aside for CBC. CBC received plenty from the Canadian taxpayer already, why should it also receive $89-million out of a total kitty of $242-million?

"We fail to understand why the public broadcaster CBC/SRC should, in addition, receive a significant contribution and guarantee from the Canadian Television Fund, which is funded primarily by the private sector," Peladeau wrote.

But the owner of Videotron had other issues as well. Videotron had been at the cutting edge of providing video on demand services in Canada, especially for French language productions.

In his letter to the CTF, Peladeau noted that "there is no justifiable reason for the Fund's failure to date to recognize the role of video on demand in the financing and dissemination of Canadian content. In Quebec alone, Illico on Demand logged nearly 20 million orders in 2006, the vast majority of which were for Canadian productions."

The reaction from CBC brass was swift. In an interview with *Le Devoir*, a left leaning newspaper with separatist sentiments, Sylvain Lafrance, the then head of French radio and television resorted to name calling.

"This guy (Péladeau) walks like a thug, and is about to derail one of the most successful television systems in the world," Lafrance said.

At first Peladeau said he was ambivalent to the remarks after a friend told him about them. Then he found out that Lafrance had repeated the statement several times in subsequent interviews.

The actual word that Peladeau claimed upset him and was damaging to his reputation was the term "*voyou*."

Depending on who is doing the translation it can be taken as punk, brat, and scofflaw or in the view of *Globe and Mail* columnist Lysanne Gagnon, Peladeau had simply been called "a bum," and it was no big deal. Gagnon might be known to English Canadians for her *Globe* columns, but in Quebec she writes for *La Presse*, a French language daily that competes with Peladeau's scrappy tabloid, *Le Journal de Montreal*.

Thug, hoodlum, punk, vandal – regardless of translation, the term was not a pleasant one.

Luc Lavoie, then a vice-president at Quebecor told the media that his company would not meet Lafrance in the gutter and then added: "It's astonishing that a bureaucrat of the Canadian state uses insults, defamation and the odious to describe the head of a great company."

The insult levied by Lafrance came after Peladeau questioned the funding of a program that his companies poured millions into but primarily benefitted CBC.

In addition to funding many of the programs put on by its competitors through contributions to the CTF, Quebecor produced many of Quebec's best loved programs. The company's TVA network held close to a 30% market share for TV audiences. This was achieved by producing homegrown versions of popular American shows and building up popular Quebec comedies and dramas.

Lance et Compte, or as we'd say in English – *He Shoots, He Scores* – was a staple on TVA. The program and the accompanying films followed the story of the fictional Quebec City hockey team, Le National. The combination of hockey, drama and risqué love stories made the show a hit that could draw more than 1.5 million viewers per week in a province with fewer than 8 million people at the time.

Peladeau invested his company's time, money and substantial effort into making shows in Quebec that Quebecers would watch. Quebecor companies contributed more to the CTF than they would receive yet, to Lafrance, Pierre Karl Peladeau was a thug intent on destroying the television system.

On top of the concerns by Peladeau and Shaw that the

Canadian Television Fund seemed like just another way to funnel money to the state broadcaster while having the private sector pick up the bill instead of government, there was a troubling report from the Auditor General, Sheila Fraser.

Studying the CTF in 2005, Fraser's office had found several problems with the program.

Yet in the eyes of one of CBC's top executives, demanding changes to a problematic program made Peladeau a thug.

Faced with what he saw as an offensive by Lafrance, and his allies, to tarnish his reputation Peladeau sued for $2.1-million. Lafrance tried to defend himself by claiming his insult wasn't aimed at Peladeau personally.

"I don't know Mr. Péladeau. I said that on this particular file, he was acting like a *voyou*," Lafrance said under questioning from Peladeau's lawyer James Woods.

The suit also named CBC president Robert Rabinovitch. Although able to speak some French, Rabinovitch didn't know the term and had to ask his assistant for a translation. He admitted under testimony that he was told voyou was a rather strong term to use.

"It's perhaps not a word one would use in polite company," Rabinovitch said.

The lawsuit, which was dropped to $700,000 by the time it went to trial, claimed that Lafrance was attempting to paint Peladeau and Quebecor as bad corporate citizens. It would be revealed in court that the decision to use the term thug to describe Peladeau was no accident.

In November 2010, the case made its way to a small room on the 15th floor of Montreal's massive courthouse, the *Palais de Justice*. Under questioning from CBC's own legal team, Lafrance explained that he and his team had made a conscious decision to attack Quebecor's stand on payments to the television fund.

Strategically they chose *Le Devoir*, the left-wing competitor to Peladeau's *Le Journal de Montreal*. Why, though, did he use the term thug? That was a question CBC lawyer Julie Chenette would ask her own client.

"I was trying to find an analogy" Lafrance said. "For me, a thug is a young person that walks around flouting the rules."

What Lafrance didn't tell the court at that point is that the rules were set up to favour his organization at the expense of Quebecor and others. The rules had been put in place in the mid-90s, didn't take into account the prevailing market realities and set aside 37% of all funds for CBC, far in excess of their market share.

For CBC the Canadian Media Fund was just another way to dip into the wallets of the Canadian public, this time through the hidden means of their cable bill: just another example of how CBC victimized the Canadian public and the cable companies that serve them.

Funding 2006-2007 Canadian Television Fund Broadcaster Performance Envelopes as of April 13, 2006 [xviv]

Total $167,232,952 for English
CTV $22,166,824
CBC $61,786,000

Total $74,847,342 for French
TVA $18,449,171
SRC $27,544,000

In the end Peladeau and Lafrance settled out of court with terms kept secret. A statement was issued which said that both sides had met and agreed it was time to "turn the page," but it did not reveal any financial settlement.

6

It Really Is Hard To Say Sorry

Claude Fournier was one of French Canada's best-known film directors and producers. Born in Waterloo, Quebec in the Eastern Townships, Fournier has more than 40 productions under his belt as a writer, director, producer, editor and cinematographer.

At the age of 74, Fournier had just finished directing a television mini-series on the life of Quebec icon Félix Leclerc. A folk singer, writer and main figure of Quebec's cultural awakening, Leclerc was revered in much of the province, especially among the cultural elite.

As a veteran of the film industry, and winner of awards from the Moscow and Montreal film festivals, Fournier was a natural to bring a mini-series on Leclerc to life for Radio-Canada. Fournier partnered with his wife Marie-Jose Raymond, an experienced producer in her own right, as well as with a writer from France, to develop the series.

While critics panned the series, as they often did with Fournier's work, audiences responded. The first night of the four-part series drew a crowd of 577,000, a healthy audience for a program aimed at Quebec's 7.5 million people. By comparison CBC's flagship program *The National* was regularly drawing a similar sized audience across all of Canada's then 32 million residents.

Then a funny thing happened. Radio-Canada attacked their own program.

Despite sinking close to $1-million into the series, plus funding from France and other sources inside the government of Canada, Mario Clement general manager of television programming at the French arm of the CBC declared to the media that the series was awful.

"It is one of the worst series I have seen on television. I didn't like the direction, the script, the choice of actors," Clement said after the first episode aired. As for the lead actor in the series, Daniel Lavoie, Clement was equally brutal.

"A good artist but he's not an actor," Clement said.

Clement claimed that he and his team at CBC had concerns all the way through the production, but claims Fournier and Raymond, would not listen to anything that was said to them.

"They despise the CBC, they despise those that they call officials of the CBC, "stated Clement. "Those people held us in scorn and made no secret of it."

Raymond laughs at the idea that she holds CBC in scorn, noting that her grandfather, Rene Morin, was president of the state broadcaster from 1940-44.

Raymond and Fournier had both worked extensively with CBC over the years and never experienced any problems.

"It is not a visceral dislike," Raymond said in a telephone interview. "I'm not someone who is against CBC. There were a lot of tries to settle before we decided to sue."

As for claims that CBC expressed concerns about the production but they were ignored, Raymond laughs at the idea.

"They paid every stage of the production. If they didn't like it, they just had to say that they wouldn't pay."

Raymond said that Mario Clement signed off on every stage of the production, but refused to meet with her or Fournier to discuss the production.

"I can show several letters asking to meet him when he took over his role," Raymond said.

Those requested meetings never occurred, and they still had not met by the time Clement let loose with his tirade against the show.

After blasting the production, Clement was asked an obvious question, why air it at all. Clement claimed that CBC was under a contractual obligation to air the program. Failure to do so would mean the producer would have to return much of the public money invested in the multi-million dollar production.

"We did not intend to put the producer in the street," Clement said.

Fournier was furious and blasted back in Montreal's *La Presse* newspaper.

"I find it disgusting. ... Why didn't Mario Clement just tell viewers to go directly to TVA? ...I never got a good review all my life. You'd think I was the punching bag of the Quebecois critics. It starts to be castrating," Fournier wrote.

Initially Fournier said he asked for a public apology, claiming that Clement went too far in attacking a series that he himself had commissioned and signed off on. When it became clear that no apology would come, Fournier sued.

His statement of claim said that the damage caused by Clement's remarks was "incalculable" and that "ostracism has inevitably been created with actors, producers and investors who will hesitate to commit themselves ... to future projects."

Fournier's court filings went on to say that the CBC executive "exceeded his mandate" when he attacked the series. "His responsibility, even contractually speaking, is to be the promoter, not the destroyer," of CBC/Radio-Canada programming.

If Fournier was looking for supporting evidence that Clement's words damaged the show and his reputation, he could easily look to the ratings. After reaching an audience of 577,000 for the first installment, the second episode pulled in just 384,000 viewers. Then there was the difficulty in lining up work in an industry where reputation is everything.

During the court proceedings, which lasted three weeks, Fournier and Raymond told the court that they had lost work because no one in the industry wanted to work with a team that had been ostracized by the powerful CBC.

The impact of his comments "was very strong in a small milieu," Raymond said.

Some productions that appeared to be moving forward with other companies were suddenly cancelled.

"When the co-producer in France sees that CBC is not only shitting on us but also that the co-production stinks and that the French are arrogant with their demands, it has an impact. We had co-producers calling and saying that they would work with Germany instead."

Star witnesses were called for both sides during the trial, with Fournier and Raymond calling former premier Lucien Bouchard and celebrated filmmaker Denys Arcand. CBC called upon the son of the late Leclerc who further disparaged the work of Fournier and Raymond. The trial lasted throughout much of March 2008, a full three years after the ordeal began.

On October 14, 2008, as most of the country was paying attention to the federal election, Justice Richard Wagner issued his ruling. Wagner said that Clement and CBC had let "frustration and obstinacy guide their behavior." He went on to say that Clement's words and actions went beyond reasonable management and were abusive.

The ruling called for CBC to pay $200,000 to Fournier and Raymond, much less than they had asked for but much more than a simple apology would have cost.

"But the CBC is a vindictive society that does not apologize," Fournier told *LaPresse* in an interview.

Despite receiving much less than hoped for, Fournier said he was glad that he fought to clear his name.

"We could have continued to let ourselves be attacked by Radio-Canada, or we could respond – we chose to respond, or at least ask for an apology, which they refused to do," he told Sun Media. "If you imagine a public apology would have been enough, you realize the public purse could have saved over a million."

CBC had spent more than $1-million defending their attacks on Fournier and Raymond. Initially the state broadcaster refused to release any documents on the costs of the lawsuit. Requests submitted by Sun Media and *LaPresse* went unanswered for four years until spring 2012. What the documents finally showed was that defending an abusive outburst and refusing to apologize had cost the taxpayers of Canada $1,074,515 in legal fees.

Money that could have gone into programming, or been put to a whole host of other constructive uses, was spent on lawyers' fees to defend a childish tirade.

7

The Song Remains The Same

On May 12, 2011, the CRTC approved the final sale of the Galaxie Music service from CBC to the privately owned Stingray Digital in Montreal. Within nine months CBC was using taxpayer's money to launch a competing online music service.

CBC may have started as a radio service and grown into a television network as well, but today the state broadcaster sees itself as a media empire that knows no bounds.

Today, CBC is a major shareholder in Sirius/XM Satellite radio, and it owns a transmission maintenance company, a mobile production company and several websites and specialty channels well outside of its mandate. These operate, with taxpayers' dollars, to compete with private sector broadcasters. In addition, CBC takes the material that Canadian taxpayers have already paid for, and then sells it to schools through its CBC Learning service.

When it comes to using tax dollars to enter the private marketplace CBC knows no shame.

How else can you explain a government owned entity selling one streaming music service to a private company and then turning around and using tax dollars to launch a competitor so soon afterwards? Yet, by April 2012, CBC had launched CBCmusic.ca, an online music service that looked eerily similar to Galaxie, but was now completely online.

CBC trumpeted the service as "Canada's free digital music service designed to connect Canadians to the music they love." The problem was that most of the music Canadians love was already being offered by players in the market, and offered either for a fee or through an advertising supported system. CBC was now offering a service that was both free and commercial free.

If CBC music was offering just the latest in Canadian content, and promoting Canadian artists, then there likely would have been no blow back. Instead though, CBC was programming dozens of online radio stations that had playlists very similar to their private sector counterparts.

From Elton John to Kelly Clarkson, Def Leppard to Toni Braxton, the music offered on the new CBC service wasn't distinct at all. Only the way it was offered was distinct – it was completely free. CBC was offering six pop channels including 70s, 80s and 90s channels, plus four stations programmed with rock music – one playing only heavy metal. It was as if CBC had taken its old Galaxie service and put it on the internet.

This service wasn't just targeting Galaxie though. CBC music was promoted as something that could be taken with you wherever you went – in the car, at work – through its mobile app for iPhones and iPads. Essentially CBC was taking aim at private radio stations that catered to people who liked pop and rock music – the kind rarely if ever heard on CBC.

This time the private broadcasters took notice. More importantly, so did Canada's music licencing body SOCAN, the group that makes sure composers and artists are paid when their music is played.

"The CBC is licenced and we need to look at the use they are making [of content] under their new service," Paul Spurgeon, vice-president of legal services at SOCAN told *The Globe and Mail.* "We're looking at that right now … the key is whether CBC is paying their fair share."

At issue was CBC's form of licence, a flat fee given their not-for-profit status. The flat-fee formula meant that CBC was paying artists less than commercial broadcasters would be required to. This licence had been fine while CBC was playing mostly classical music, the odd bit of folk and jazz and even running shows that promoted obscure Canadian artists. Now, though, they were running a full-fledged commercial-style operation as if they were a top 40 radio station.

Jim Cuddy, one of the two front men for the band Blue Rodeo, said with CBC running a new kind of service, their former status should change.

"As there is a new format [live-streaming] and the CBC is currently paying a nominal fee, it only seems fair that a new rate be negotiated," Cuddy told the *Globe.*

That was on March 11, less than a month after the service was launched. A month later it was the broadcaster's turn and they too took issue with CBC's preferential royalty rate – a rate granted CBC due to its status as a not-for-profit government entity.

"The CBC is using the preferential royalty rates it receives from the various collective societies because of its status as a non-profit public broadcaster to make the service viable in the long term," a coalition of broadcasters wrote in a letter to Heritage Minister James Moore.

"We ask that the CBC be compelled to justify its actions and explain how the launch of the CBC Music service is not competitive with existing services offered by private broadcasters and how it is not damaging to the industry."

The group, led by Stingray, also included Quebecor, which owned the recently launched service Zik.ca, Cogeco Cable, the Jim Pattison Group and Golden West Radio.

The letter took note of the fact that, in addition to targeting online services like Galaxie and Zik, this new service was also squarely aimed at the private radio market.

CBC helped bring Sirius Satellite Radio to Canada in 2005 by putting millions of taxpayers' dollars at risk. Canada's government-owned broadcaster was once again competing with the private sector.

Among the channels CBC helped bring to Canada – Howard Stern, Playboy and Spice Radio. Spice is an "adult" channel featuring shows such as *Strippertown, You Porn* and *Wives Cheat*.

"These actions further distance the corporation from its mandate, while placing it directly on a collision course with private broadcasters who can only rely on advertising and subscription revenues to sustain their services."

The complaint likely fell on deaf ears. Moore had long been a champion of CBC, defending the state broadcaster and its mission creep inside a Conservative Party caucus that was skeptical of the organization. In fact before the complaints came in, Moore had already proclaimed his love for the service.

"CBC Music, a great addition to programming, has gone well. I think the CBC will be fine," Moore gushed to CBC's George Stroumboulopoulos during a television appearance to talk about cuts to the CBC budget.

That view wasn't sitting well with the private sector. Companies that had invested their own money to build music services were now watching a government-owned body compete with them for the Elton John and Kelly Clarkson audience.

"Our problem is that these are taxpayer dollars which are being used to compete against private industry," said Rob Braide, vice-president of Stingray.

"When you play a song on the radio or the internet or on television, the person that wrote that song and quite often the artist and the record label are paid a fee," Braide said of the complicated royalty structure. "When that service [CBC music] is not 100% Canadian, it means that those rights that the corporation is paying are going to Elton John and Lady Gaga. They're not staying on shore to promote Great Lake Swimmers and Canadian music."

Braide said CBC was trying to convince the Canadian public that music could be had for free.

"They are trying to say that music is free and music isn't free, we have to pay our artists or they die," Braide said.

The coalition of private broadcasters asked Moore to shut the service down, or force them to operate on a level playing field with higher royalties and by charging a fee. Alternatively they asked that the service be made a Canadian music service.

"Let's make it a Canadian service, a 100% Canadian service and let's pay copyright dollars to Canadian artists instead of Elton John and Lady Gaga," Braide said.

CBC's response to the charges against them was complete denial.

Despite everyone in the industry knowing that they pay a preferential rate based on their status, the state broadcaster denied this special arrangement existed.

"First off, CBC Music does not receive any preferential treatment when we negotiate our rights deals," read a letter posted to their site in response to the criticism. "Just like everyone else, the nature of the services we offer is examined (either by the Copyright Board or the party we are negotiating with) and then rates are set – or negotiated – accordingly."

"On the question of whether CBC Music should be "competing" in the same space as private broadcasters, I think it's safe to say that each one of you knows CBC Music does not exist to compete, it exists to serve; Canadians, musicians and our cultural community."

The letter was signed by Chris Boyce, Mark Steinmetz and Steve Pratt, three executives with the service. They encouraged fans to write into the CRTC in support of the "role we play in the Canadian music ecosystem." The appeal was big on the importance of Canadian music to CBC's online offerings without mentioning that most of what had been added was the same commercial music offered everywhere else – the kind normally mocked on CBC airwaves.

8

Where Success Is A Firing Offence

"We are parting ways," CBC president Hubert Lacroix announced.

With that short sentence Richard Stursberg was fired as the top executive for English television and radio at the Canadian Broadcasting Corporation. Stursberg wasn't fired for doing a bad job; quite the opposite, he was fired for doing a good job and attempting to make CBC less elitist than it was.

Stursberg had taken the CBC from an average minute audience of 215,000 when he took the helm in late 2004 to an audience of 328,000 for the 12 months prior to his departure in the summer of 2010. Yet, despite increasing the average number of eyeballs watching CBC at any given minute by 52% and increasing overall market share by 34%, Stursberg was out.[xx]

His only crime was rocking the boat at the staid old CBC. In attempting to push the state broadcaster to achieve bigger and better things, to produce shows Canadians cared about, he was fired and became another victim of the CBC.

Prior to joining CBC, Stursberg had spent his entire life in Canada's government sponsored arts organizations: Executive Director of Telefilm Canada, Chair of the Canadian Television Fund and assistant deputy minister for Culture and Broadcasting. There had been a bit of time in the private sector as CEO of the upstart satellite company Star choice (Now Shaw Satellite), and as president of the Canadian Cable Television Association, but mainly Richard Stursberg worked for government arts bodies.

Still, when he was approached to head up CBC's English radio and television services, Stursberg knew there were problems.

As part of his effort to better understand how the entire system operated, Stursberg told Tony Burman, then head honcho for news, that he wanted to set up a desk in the newsroom that would let him work there from time to time and get to know people.

Burman blew his stack telling Stursberg that having the boss around would intimidate the journalists. Yes, the very same people that CBC expected to question the most powerful people in the country would be intimidated by their boss showing up in the office.

Doesn't leave you with a good impression does it?

Prior to taking the job Stursberg asked then president of the CBC, Robert Rabinovitch, "Who does it serve?"

Stursberg wanted to know what the point of the CBC was.

"Is the CBC there to serve the chatterati, the cultural elites – or the public at large? Is it supposed to make art-house fare or Canadian entertainment shows that Canadians might actually find entertaining?"[xxi]

For continually asking that question over the next six years and pushing CBC, Stursberg would eventually be fired.

Ratings were at a 30 year low in 2004. Canadians had abandoned CBC programming, and not just in their desire to be entertained: CBC News had fallen from the dominant position it once held to third spot nationally behind CTV and Global.

Stursberg had been leading Telefilm Canada and attempting the seemingly impossible task of getting English speaking Canadians to watch Canadian made film. The goal at Telefilm was to see English language Canadian films capture 5% of the box-office.

It was a huge task, but with popular fare such as *Bon Cop, Bad Cop* and *Pashcendale* in the works, there was some small hope that Telefilm could hit that mark. Like CBC, Telefilm was part of the Canadian cultural elite: those taxpayer funded bodies that would take millions of dollars from hard working Canadians and then produce shows and films most people didn't want to watch.

Stursberg was of the mind that more Canadians should actually want to watch Canadian programs even if that meant making less "art-house fare" and funding projects with a wider audience potential. This alone made the executive controversial in the cultural welfare community.

To those who live on the dole of arts grants and the complex web of funding arrangements for movies and TV, making something popular means selling out. Even if the people pay for it, they shouldn't understand it nor have a say as to what gets produced.

Stursberg had different ideas, and with ratings at the state broadcaster at an all-time low, this was the very reason Rabinovitch wanted to bring him in. Even as he contemplated joining, Stursberg knew that turning around the CBC would be a mammoth task.

"The CBC's legendary inability to meet the most elementary test of good management, and its soft left, anti-business, Toronto-centric, politically correct cultural assumptions created significant problems for the corporation," Stursberg wrote in his memoirs.

Taking on the complacent nature of CBC's management and the less than entrepreneurial nature of the staff would be a huge challenge.

One of the many things to shock Stursberg when he took over the CBC was how little people inside the corporation knew about their own situation. Staff was aware that the newly minted boss cared about ratings, and considered whether people watched your programs to be a measure of success, but few inside CBC knew what the ratings for their shows were.

Despite every major television broadcaster in the country having access to overnight ratings detailing the ups and downs of Canadian viewing habits, Stursberg found that CBC staff were mostly in the dark about their ratings. They were, after all, producing programs in keeping with CBC's "mandate," and of a higher quality than the material being produced by those lowly private broadcasters. Ratings didn't matter for such programs.

Or at least that was the thinking.[xxii]

So when Stursberg suggested to producers at *The National*, the flagship newscast of the state broadcaster, that he would like to see them pulling in around 750,000 viewers per night, they had no idea what the challenge was. They hadn't seen the ratings since management had purposely kept that information secret.

The National was a last place newscast in the three-way race, but few seemed to know the exact figures. Neither did the people making the program or its local counterparts in cities across Canada know WHY they were losing out to Global and CTV. One of the shocking things Stursberg found, travelling to different newsrooms across Canada, is that nobody bothered to watch their competition to get tips on why they might be beating them night after night. Instead all CBC newsroom TVs were tuned to CBC or BBC.[xxiii]

As he began planning changes to turn CBC's fortunes around, Stursberg was met with incredible resistance.

Antonia Zerbisias, the media columnist for the *Toronto Star*, referred to CBC's new head of programming as a disaster. "Since he joined the CBC in the fall of 2004, Stursberg has been a one-man wrecking ball." Zerbisias wrote. "Morale at the CBC is at an all-time low."

The *Globe and Mail*'s TV critic John Doyle began referring to CBC headquarters as "Fort Dork."

The hostility to making changes at the state broadcaster was not just being driven by angry TV critics upset that the schedule of their favourite, if little watched, shows were being adjusted. No, the hostility came from deep inside the belly of the beast.

Employees of CBC began leaking memos or directives issued by Stursberg to other media outlets, hoping that bad coverage from the likes of Zerbisias, Doyle and other charter members of what is described as "The Constituency" would stop the changes.

When he had begun thinking about taking the job, one of the first things Stursberg asked was, "Who does it serve?" Obviously some members of "The Constituency" felt the job of the state broadcaster was to serve the "chatterati and cultural elites," and not the public at large.

One of Stursberg's decisions to encourage more Canadians to actually watch CBC programs was to not only commission the production of entertaining shows, but also to air programs in their best time slots. When it was announced that *the fifth estate* would be moving from Wednesday to Friday there was outrage. *The Walrus*, a downtown Toronto-centric lefty magazine – the kind perfect for CBC's internal audience – declared that the investigative news program was being shuffled to "...the graveyard of television." Program host Linden McIntyre declared the end: "Gone, all gone," he said.

Instead the show's ratings went up.

While the mucky-mucks who had run the CBC into the ground didn't like the change, or that *the fifth estate* was being moved to make room for a show called, *Being Erica*, regular Canadians did. Immediately the audience grew from 525,000 to 630,000 and by the end of the season had grown further.[xxiv]

Being Erica also turned out to be a hit.

If shuffling schedules appeared to be difficult for Stursberg in an attempt to get people watching again, bringing balance to the slant of news casts would be even harder.

CBC has its own culture, which at times appears to involve highly educated people who all think the same about any given issue holding up a mirror in front of their faces and then declaring that the image they see represents Canada. One former CBC staff member tells of being in a story meeting where the Harper government's tough on crime agenda was raised. As the journalists and producers kicked the story around each of them expressed dismay that anyone would think there was a need to get tough on crime. Finally a senior reporter spoke up, "You need to remember that unlike us, some people actually believe that criminals should be punished."

Others who have spent time in the news department at CBC describe an environment that is fully hostile to anything that could be construed as conservative. During the 2006 federal election campaign, one CBC television reporter regularly referred to the Conservatives and Stephen Harper's team as "those fuckers." Neither their CBC colleagues nor the rest of the Parliamentary press pack batted an eye at the description.

In short, CBC was so left wing, they couldn't recognize the right any longer except as an enemy.

It was in this environment that Stursberg would attempt to bring some balance.

As he explained to government insiders worried about the slant and bias of CBC, the question wasn't whether Judy Rebick the one-time darling of the militant left was on CBC but also whether Ezra Levant was on.

Indeed Levant was on, prior to the launch of Sun News Network, but not without controversy.

Even more controversial though was Stursberg's recruitment of Kory Teneycke, the former director of communications for Prime Minister Stephen Harper and the man behind the launch of Sun News.

"He is very clever, very right-wing and very articulate. He was ideal for television," Stursberg wrote.

Not everyone agreed.

New Democrat MP Charlie Angus, the NDP culture critic, slammed the hiring of Teneycke in the halls of Parliament. Why would the CBC do such a thing, Angus wondered? He went so far as to write a letter to CBC's ombudsman, claiming Teneycke's hiring as a political commentator violated CBC's own written code of standards.

"Mr. Teneycke has also demonstrated very little ability to provide political commentary that demonstrates anything but a bias toward the Conservative Party of Canada," Angus wrote in May 2010.

Having partisan Liberals or New Democrats on CBC was acceptable, but to many inside the state broadcaster, Teneycke was completely unacceptable. Fights raged in CBC's Ottawa bureau after many of Teneycke's appearances and the CBC's biggest supporters rebelled.

The Globe and Mail, which had ignored CBC as a place to perform investigative journalism on how tax dollars were spent, actually filed an access to information request on Teneycke's terms of employment. The salary of Peter Mansbridge – purported to be in the range of $750,000 – the spending habits of senior executives and other expenses at CBC were of no interest to Canada's self-described paper of record, but the part-time earnings of a political commentator were.

9

Taxpayers Of Canada, The Repeat Victims

The biggest victim of the CBC, on an ongoing basis, might just be the Canadian taxpayer.

It is true that CBC has not defamed or run down the reputation of the Canadian taxpayer the way they have with people like Dr. Frans Leenen, Marie-Jose Raymond, Brian Mulroney or Peter Nygard, but taxpayers are victims.

In the ten years prior to CBC coming under the Access to Information Act in September 2007, taxpayers forked over $11.5-billion to CBC and had very little understanding of how that money was spent. Sure, they knew that the money went to run a television and radio network but, unlike the money given to the military, there was no openness about spending at CBC.

Acting on a campaign promise to open up the books at CBC, the Canadian Wheat Board and dozens of other organizations that received taxpayers' dollars, the Harper Conservatives introduced and passed a bill that put these organizations under the same rules as other government departments. Well almost the same rules: CBC was given a special exclusion.

To allay fears that journalistic sources or actors pay rates might be released Parliament included what is now known as section 68.1 of the Access to Information Act.

> 68.1 This Act does not apply to any information that is under the control of the Canadian Broadcasting Corporation that relates to its journalistic, creative or programming activities, other than information that relates to its general administration.

Now, a normal reading of the act would say that finding out what CBC paid for its newest shows, or what stories journalists are working on, would be blocked, but inquiring about how many vehicles CBC operated would qualify for access to information. Yet, CBC used clause 68.1 to turn down a simple request to detail how many vehicles they owned or leased.

The documents released by the state broadcaster were mostly blank pages – with one exception, a lone Ford 500 sedan. The claim was simply unbelievable, that a coast to coast network that operates in two languages ran on just one sedan. Of course, that's not what CBC was claiming, but that one car was all they would admit to.

In denying information about any other vehicles, CBC relied on their exclusion under the act. They actually claimed that telling the public who pays their bills how many cars and trucks they owned or leased was an infringement on their "journalistic, creative or programming activities." It took almost a year after the denial of records was published in Sun Media newspapers for CBC to finally admit that they had a fleet of 728 vehicles.

This single vehicle claim is not CBC's only abuse of the access to information system in their ongoing attempts to keep the public from knowing how taxpayers' money is spent. As mentioned earlier, a request regarding the costs of the court case involving Marie-Jose Raymond was stonewalled for several years. That case cost taxpayers more than $1-million in settlement and legal fees when it could have been settled with an apology. If CBC is going to waste taxpayers money defending lawsuits they will ultimately lose, then the people paying the bill should be able to find out the true cost.

In some ways, though, it is remarkable that the public knows any costs.

CBC was given plenty of warning that they would be coming under the Access to Information Act. The change required new policies, new staff, training and plenty of organization. It also apparently involved plenty of shredding.

CBC actually admitted that, in preparation for coming under the act, they spent a considerable sum for shredding services. It's not known what exactly was shredded but documents released by CBC show that they did spend $60,000 on shredding services in the months leading up to their new "open" status taking effect.

Another tactic CBC used was to be as vague as possible with anything put to paper. Guy Fournier who served as chairman of the CBC board of directors says minutes of meetings he was at were incomprehensible.

"At one point the minutes of the board were so vague that even members couldn't say whether they were right. They were absolutely meaningless," Fournier said.

When he complained and asked that future minutes offer great clarity, he was told that, with the state broadcaster coming under the access law, the plan was to keep the minutes vague enough that no one would be able to understand anything by reading them.

Beyond shredding and being vague, CBC did its best to block the release of information. In fact CBC was so good at not releasing information that they received repeat failing grades from the federal information commissioner. In her 2009-2010 annual report, Commissioner Suzanne Legault noted that in the previous year she had received 1,095 complaints of

In 2006 the Harper Conservatives won election with a promise to bring CBC and 69 other agencies and crown corporations under the access to information act. CBC knew their time was coming and they prepared by shredding documents. An access to information request for the "shredding of records in anticipation of CBC/SRC being subjected to the Access to Information Act" turned up an interesting fact.

The state broadcaster spent $59,160 shredding documents and destroying records in 2006 in preparation for their time in the limelight.

What was shredded?

That remains a protected mystery.

which 889 were levied against CBC. In her next report, CBC was given an F grade for their handling of access requests.

While access to information requests are often used by media outlets, political parties and professional researchers, the premise of the system is that any Canadian should be able to fill out a simple form, pay their $5 fee and find out how a government department is spending taxpayers' dollars. It's a simple and wonderful idea: those paying the bills should be able to find out how that money is spent. Yet with CBC, it hasn't worked out this way.

From requests on how much employee absenteeism costs taxpayers to the amount taxpayers shell out to rent office space, the brass at CBC have found ways to get around releasing financial information.

In one case CBC refused to release the cost of a cleaning and maintenance contract. The contract was awarded to Profac, a subsidiary of SNC-Lavalin, and should have been subjected to normal disclosure rules. Similar contracts between the same company and the federal Department of Public Works had shown serious problems. In one instance, in the Public Works contracts taxpayers were billed $5,000 for installing six lights, while in another case, they were dinged $1,000 for replacing a doorbell.

When the story broke it caused a mini-sensation on Parliament Hill and raised questions about building maintenance and contracting practices. The contract contained clauses limiting maintenance work during the day resulting in large overtime bills for after-hours calls. Did the CBC contract have similar clauses? Taxpayers couldn't find out. CBC refused to release their contract with Profac, claiming it was confidential business information.

CBC's determination to keep its secrets secret eventually led to a court case. Acting on complaints from several sources that CBC was being too secretive with how it spent taxpayers' money, Commissioner Legault asked CBC to allow her to review 16 files that had been subject to their special exclusion. Legault wanted to test the 16 files to see if CBC was only excluding material of a "journalistic, creative or programming" nature, or if they were also excluding information on CBC's general administration which was not excluded from the law.

Among the files to be tested was a request to find out the total amount that CBC paid in fees while filing access to information requests with other government departments, the cost of a contest to select a replacement

---

CBC claimed they could not release information that was journalistic or program-related. Here are some of the requests they rejected that became part of the court case

Theme song. *Hockey Night in Canada*. Provide records on the cost of running the contest to find the new *Hockey Night in Canada* theme song

We wish to have access to or a copy of all and/or any records regarding spending by CBC on advertising in the greater Montreal area. Specifically advertising in the form of visual media, i.e. Billboards, print ads, buses, etc

Provide copy of all records concerning the handover of the position of the CEO from Mr. Robert Rabinovitch to Mr. Hubert T. Lacroix

Statutory fees paid by CBC for the submission of ATI requests. Provide a copy of records indicating the amount of fees paid pursuant to the federal access to information statute during Fiscal Year 2007-2008.

theme song for *Hockey Night in Canada* and the cost of advertising in Montreal. If Legault found that CBC was improperly applying their exclusion, she could order the files to be released. Then again if she found their practices within the law then they would stay secret.

CBC refused to comply with Legault's request to examine the files, and challenged her in court.

The irony seemed lost on CBC.

The news organization that demanded openness and accountability from every other government department was refusing to submit to that same standard. The news organization that would scream at cabinet ministers and business executives, "What are you hiding?", was now hiding.

Beyond hiding, CBC was actively challenging an independent officer of Parliament. Although not as well known, the position of Information Commissioner is on a level-footing with that of the Auditor General. Both report to Parliament, and not simply to the government of the day. Both have extraordinary powers to hold the government to account. Yet here was CBC refusing to comply.

To be clear, CBC was not the first government department to challenge the information commissioner in court – and it won't be the last. Yet there was something strange about an organization that had reporters dogging the government of the day over transparency, and the releasing of documents now refusing even to allow the information commissioner to examine their books.

Here's how commissioner Legault described the situation to the House of Commons Standing Committee on Access to Information, Privacy and Ethics in October of 2011:

"In the course of our investigations, we asked the CBC to provide us with information that had been withheld so that we could assess whether its decision on disclosure was justified or whether the withheld information fell within the exception to the exclusion. The CBC refused to provide the relevant information and so my office issued a production order to the CBC in relation to certain complaints.

That same day, the Corporation initiated a judicial review application under s. 18 of the Federal Courts Act challenging my Office's authority to obtain records they claimed were excluded under s. 68.1."

The Federal Court found in favour of Legault and her office, but CBC appealed. When MPs questioned Lacroix as to why he was using taxpayers' dollars to fight an officer of Parliament in court, he was utterly dismissive.

"We believe that only a judge should have the right to demand the disclosure of information that relates to our creative activities or is journalistic or program related," Lacroix told the Commons access committee in March of 2011.

CBC once claimed that the travel and hospitality expenses of one executive, Louise Lantange, were completely off limits. The state broadcaster claimed that Lantange's expenses were exempted under section 68.1 as expenses related to journalistic, creative or programming resources.

"As general manager for *Television de Radio-Canada*, Louise Lantagne's activities and related expenses are most of the time deeply intertwined with our programming activities," said CBC spokesman Marco Dube.

Yes because knowing how many four martini lunches an executive has on our dime might spill the beans on what shows CBC is going to buy.

The implication in those words, "only a judge," meant that even the members of Parliament that voted on CBC's annual billion dollar plus subsidy, who passed the laws that governed how the state broadcaster should operate, were not of a high enough order to look at how CBC spends taxpayers dollars. In a sense, Lacroix had appeared before the very people that paid his bills and flipped them the bird.

Had Lacroix's viewpoint eventually won the day, it would have meant that any citizen who wanted information from CBC would have to be willing to take them to court to get it. This is supposed to be a system that allows ordinary Canadians to get a peek at how government works. CBC's plan was to make sure that this system was so bogged down in legal proceedings that it would never work.

Lacroix's arrogance on this file would lead to a showdown a few months later when after the May 2, 2011 election, the Conservatives held a majority on the access committee and demanded to see some of the documents CBC was withholding.

After hearing from Legault and Quebecor president Pierre Karl Peladeau on CBC's shoddy record on access to information, the Conservative MPs on the committee, led by Peterborough MP Dean Del Mastro, demanded that several files be handed over so that MPs could examine the documents as part of their study on the issue. Immediately the opposition parties and much of the media went to bat to protect CBC and its secrets.

People who had previously demanded the full release of documents related to Taliban prisoners in Afghanistan were now saying that Parliament could not possibly be trusted to look at internal documents of the state broadcaster, even if it were done behind closed doors.

Rob Walsh, the Parliamentary law clerk had issued a legal opinion in December 2009, stating that the Commons defence committee could see whatever documents it wanted while studying the mission to Afghanistan.

"As I indicated in my earlier letter," Walsh wrote on the Afghan file, "it is important to remember that the committee, charged by the House with reviewing Canada's mission in Afghanistan, is at all times to be seen as carrying out its constitutional function of holding the Government to account. The law of parliamentary privilege provides that this relationship operates unencumbered by legal constraints that might otherwise seem applicable."

Less than two years later, Walsh was warning the Conservatives not to look into CBC documents because it might be illegal to do so.

CBC initially balked at handing over any documents, despite their own reporters having said countless times on television and radio that Parliamentary committees can demand the production of any document they wished to see. What applies to national security files apparently did not apply to CBC records. The fight was on.

"I think they understand that they've got a committee order to produce documents, I just cannot imagine that the public broadcaster is going to refuse to release documents to an in camera committee meeting," Del Mastro told reporters at the time.

Del Mastro insisted that, if CBC refused to hand over the documents, they would be in contempt of Parliament.

CBC handed over some files in a sealed envelope and asked the committee not to look at them. At that time, they also released to the public the aforementioned records on their vehicle fleet. That document revealed the true size of their fleet as 728 vehicles at the time of the initial request. It also showed that CBC had been overly zealous in how it applied its exception provision to the new access to information law as a way to guard its secrets.

A week after the drama on Parliament Hill, CBC once again lost in court. The federal court of appeal ruled that the information commissioner did have the right to examine the documents it had requested to see if the law was being properly applied.

CBC's initial reaction to the loss was to say they were considering their options, including an appeal all the way to the Supreme Court. Public sentiment, however, was not on their side. A poll released two months earlier had already shown that 64% of Canadians thought it was wrong for the state broadcaster to use tax dollars to fight an officer of Parliament in federal court. That view ran across all party lines.

After some thought, CBC conceded defeat and announced that they would abide by the ruling and work with the information commissioner in the future. That doesn't mean that CBC has become a pillar of openness.

Requests for information from CBC regularly invoke other sections of the Access to Information Act as a way to keep secrets from being released to the public. CBC, which bristles at the term state broadcaster, has no qualms over invoking section 18, which allows information vital to the economic interests of Canada to be withheld. They are also quite fond of section 21:

21. (1) The head of a government institution may refuse to disclose any record requested under this Act that contains

(a) advice or recommendations developed by or for a government institution or a minister of the Crown,...

It boggles the mind that CBC claims not to be a state broadcaster, but then relies on sections of the act that use all of the trappings of government to stop the great unwashed from finding out its secrets.

10

Living The High Life On Your Dime

While CBC worked hard at keeping their secrets under wraps, attacking those who sought openness from the state broadcaster, some information on spending did come out, and it wasn't a pretty picture.

Before the bright glare of public scrutiny changed their ways, executives at the state broadcaster were living the lifestyle of the rich and famous using the money provided by John and Jane Canuck. It seemed that the name of the game was spend and spend fast.

One of the worst offenders was Sylvain Lafrance, the head of CBC's French language services.

For flights that would last 40 minutes between Montreal,

Toronto and Ottawa, Lafrance racked up business class fares of $1,000 per flight. One Montreal to Toronto return flight set taxpayers back $1,109.43 while a flight to St. John's, Newfoundland cost hardworking Canadians $2,620.07.

Bet you didn't know there were so many Francophone's in St. John's.

Lafrance's high-flying lifestyle wasn't restricted to Canada. In 2008, he spent $4,821.09 on flights that included a 48-hour stopover in Paris. Flights for a three day trip inflicted $5,802.70 worth of damage on taxpayers. Of course those amounts don't include food, drinks, hotels or limo rides.

Whether the expense was high or low, Lafrance made sure that taxpayers were footing the bill for his lifestyle. Everything from a $309 dinner in Paris to a $1.65 muffin in Ottawa was expensed by the vice-president of the CBC. Among the interesting items taxpayers paid for – boozy lunches with other CBC staff.

Lafrance wasn't opposed to treating others to a pricey meal or a few drinks, and then sticking us with the tab. That included others already at the government trough, including other CBC employees and even a Senator. In October 2009, Lafrance billed taxpayers for a $119

At the time of writing a non-stop flight from Montreal to Paris complete with a three night stay at the luxurious Hotel d'Louvre could be had for just $2,267. The same flight but with just 4 star accommodation could be had starting at $1,198.

That's a far cry from the $5,802.70 that Lafrance billed taxpayers simply for flights.

lunch. That luncheon featured just Lafrance and one guest, Liberal Senator Francis Fox. It isn't clear what business the two could possibly have together. Fox was an opposition Senator with no sway over CBC budgets or administration. In fact Fox hadn't held any real political sway since 1978 when he was forced to resign from his position as solicitor-general in Pierre Trudeau's cabinet after being caught forging the signature of his girlfriend's husband to help her get an abortion.

Still Lafrance and Fox, both already drawing hefty government paycheques, sat down to nosh and drink while using other people's money. There was no itemized bill released for the meal, but a review of the restaurant's online menu showed that lunch was under $20 per person meaning that, at $119, the two likely knocked back quite a few drinks with their meal.

A couple of key examples show that Lafrance, who has since left CBC, might have been at his most comfortable spending tax dollars to eat and drink with his colleagues. An access to information request on a 2006 executive retreat showed that Canadians paid for $1,400 worth of booze on what was supposed to be a two-day working retreat at Les Trois Tilleuls et Spa Givenchy. This resort was 35 minutes from their Montreal offices.

The 12 hotel rooms for the retreat cost $6,800, while dining room costs at the four-star inn totalled $2,056. Detailed receipts, which are no longer released, show that a late dinner bill totalled $825, with only $146 going to food. The rest went to eight bottles of wine, eight glasses of wine, one whisky sour and nine bottles of sparkling and flat water. Tap water apparently isn't good enough for the folks at CBC.

A review of expense claims released under access to information and proactive disclosure figures put out by

CBC suggest that Lafrance spent more than $38,000 on travel expenses and entertainment in 2007, and more than $39,000 in 2008. That works out to more than $100 in expenses for every single day of the year on top of his already hefty salary.

Exactly how much Lafrance earned in salary while at CBC is hard to discern. The state broadcaster may use public money to pay for salaries and bonuses, but they don't believe the public has any right to know what level the executive compensation sits at. That is in stark contrast to private sector companies that are publicly traded on stock exchanges. Those companies are required to give detailed reports on executive compensation.

At CBC, salaries remain a mystery and bonuses are given within a general range.

In the fiscal year that ended on March 31, 2008, CBC's 12 member executive team split just shy of $1-million. That exact figure, $964,860 was close to 10% of the annual operational subsidy given to the state broadcaster that year, and only 12 of the nearly 10,000 employees split those funds. CBC defended the bonuses as a cost of doing business while competing for talent with private broadcasters.

"There is a salary component and an incentive component and given the size of the organization, the

In 2006 the average Canadian worker would have to work more than 60 hours to earn enough money to pay for all the booze CBC executives consumed during a two-day retreat. Of course that 60 hours of work would only pay for all the booze if there was no tax taken off to pay for things like CBC. In reality the average Canadian worker would have to work two weeks full-time to pay for one boozy CBC weekend.

budgets that are administered, the number of people that are managed, you have to have a compensation package that allows you to attract and retain not only competent but talented management," spokesman Jeff Keay told the *Toronto Sun*.

Not everyone was buying that line.

"We object to the idea that it's OK for a Crown corporation [CBC] to act like a private entity when it comes to executive compensation," Adam Taylor, acting federal director of the Canadian Taxpayers Federation told the *Sun*. "In a time when tax revenue will be scarce, this should outrage ordinary Canadians."

Heritage Minister James Moore distanced himself from the bonuses through a spokesperson who told the *Sun* that, "CBC is responsible for their own day to day business."

The next year it would be tougher for Moore to distance himself from the generous bonuses, try as he might.

In the fall of 2008, the economic turmoil that had been rocking the United States began to hit Canada hard. Job losses started mounting in October of that year, consumer spending collapsed, and fear took hold. As could be expected in the middle of so much economic turmoil, ad revenues for media companies plummeted as consumers and businesses tightened spending.

With the drop in revenue came a drop in the number of employees media companies carried. One by one, companies announced layoffs and cost cutting programs. As jobs were shed many media organizations also cut company travel plans, eliminated management bonuses or stopped planning raises.

Not CBC.

The state broadcaster, like all broadcasters was feeling the pinch of the soft advertising market. Few companies were advertising and those that were had cut their ad budgets significantly. This chipped away at the revenue CBC generated from its television stations to supplement the billion dollars given to them by taxpayers.

While other companies cut, CBC asked the government for more money, tens of millions of dollars more. The government refused, citing a weak economy, declining tax revenue and the realities of the market. CBC announced that it would cut 800 jobs to make up for their shortfall.

The one thing they didn't cut was the executive bonuses.

In March 2009, a month where 61,000 Canadians lost their jobs in the middle of the worst recession since the 1930s, CBC's top ten executives split a bonus kitty worth $888,699. The top bonus paid out that year was $165,090, but it is not clear who that money went to. CBC refused to release the names when they released the bonus list.

The decision to pay huge bonuses while cutting staff was noticed by MPs.

"Is it appropriate for CBC to be spending on bonuses when people are being laid off?", asked Conservative MP Dean Del Mastro during a Commons committee hearing.

If CBC's executives split their 2008 bonuses equally in true CBC/socialist style, then each executive would have taken home $80,405 each. Or put another way, their bonuses would have been nearly double what the average Canadian earned that year. And don't forget the bonus is on top of their hefty paycheques.

Del Mastro had put the question to CBC president Hubert Lacroix, who said bonuses are necessary because executive pay is "below market." Lacroix added that CBC used the incentive to "try to bring back our executive pay to a certain level." Conservative MPs were especially unhappy with the situation. In total, some 553 managers or five percent of CBC workforce were eligible for bonuses at the time, and were collecting them even as the pink slips were being handed out to the employees they managed.

Under pressure from Conservative members of the committee, Lacroix said that bonuses would be cut between 20 percent and 50 percent in the following year, and would save the state broadcaster $4-million. It isn't known if those cuts were made to the bonus pay of the middle and lower ends of CBC's sea of managers, but senior executives were let off easy. In the year that ended March 31, 2010, CBC's top ten senior executives split a $778,799 bonus kitty, a drop of just over 12 percent – taxpayer money being used to treat so-called public servants like stars.

In the most recent round of CBC cuts, the ones where Russian and Portuguese language programming aimed at foreign countries was eliminated, Lacroix also announced hundreds of new job cuts. Asked during an online discussion with employees whether senior executive bonuses would be cut he simply replied, "No." At CBC the executives are entitled to their entitlements and you are entitled to pay for them.

Are you able to bill your boss $100 per day in extra expenses above and beyond what you get on your paycheque?

Paying for their entitlements doesn't end with big salaries and huge bonuses; it also extends to some nifty perks. Those precise perks are a monthly car allowance, club memberships, residential security system installation, child/elder care, health care spending accounts, registered education savings plans, a flexible component of the CBC pension, financial planning and parking.

Documents released under access to information, which stripped out the cost of all of these perks for CBC's top executives, also listed clothing allowances and spousal travel benefits. CBC, however, denies those are ever paid out, or that executives are even eligible for them. "I want to make clear that CBC/Radio-Canada executives have never been eligible for clothing allowance or spousal travel. CBC/Radio-Canada executives are indeed eligible for a perquisite program that can be applied to a precise list of eligible categories," spokesman Angus McKinnon told Sun Media.

Even without a clothing allowance or spousal benefits, the perks enjoyed by CBC executives are out of reach of almost all the Canadians who pay their bills. Most Canadians don't get their daycare paid by their employer, or work for a company that will hire a nurse to check in on their ailing mother. Most Canadians don't get their golf memberships paid for, let alone the installation of

Nothing says you are the people's broadcaster quite like pocketing a bonus of $165,090 while hundreds of thousands of others are losing their jobs. That mega bonus was equal to roughly 3.5 times what the average Canadian earned in 2009. Of course it was much, much more than what the hundreds of thousands who lost their jobs earned that year.

a security system for their personal residence. For most Canadians those costs of living need to come out of their paycheques, paycheques which are significantly smaller than the ones taken home by Hubert Lacroix and his team.

Yes, indeed, Canadian taxpayers are among victims of the CBC.

Did you even know that Canada ever had a radio service in Russian or Portuguese? We did. It wasn't really aimed at Canadian audiences, it was an overseas type service. Don't worry though, if you like paying for foreign radio you are still paying for CBC to run Spanish, Chinese and Arabic programming plus an English and French service aimed at people who live outside of Canada.

Hubie salary range
$358,400 and $421,600
$34,000 – $56,500 chauffeur
$30,000 expenses in 2011
Bonus? Up to 50% of salary

Being a CBC executive allows you to treat your friends to secret lunches. On March 31, 2011, CBC President Hubert Lacroix billed taxpayers $242.47 for a simple lunch of soup, club sandwiches and soft drinks.

Why did the lunch cost so much?

Lacroix held his simple luncheon at the exclusive Mount Royal Club. As if eating lunch at a swanky private club were not enough Lacroix rented a private room to make the affair even more intimate. So who was the guest? CRTC Chair Konrad von Finckenstein, the man then in charge of Canada's broadcast regulator.

11

Did You Know?

CBC Party-Hearty at Tax Payer's Expense

In September 2011, CBC was exposed for having billed taxpayers for a big exclusive party. Bono from U2, Jon Hamm from the hit TV show *Mad Men* and Kiefer Sutherland were among the guests invited by CBC's George Stroumboulopoulos to a party at the swanky Hazelton Hotel. The hotel bills itself as "Toronto, Canada's most exclusive five-star hotel." CBC stuck you with the bill for the event and refused for months to release any costs.

"That's not something we would share with you," CBC spokesman Jeff Keay said when asked about the cost. Keay claimed that the information was of a competitive nature and would not be released.

The reason for the party was the Toronto International Film Festival and the desire by Stroumboulopoulos to hang out with cool people.

"I've always wanted to be in a band, not a solo artist," Stroumboulopoulos said. "And I want to be in a community. I've always thought that community is interesting. An individual is a tree. A group of individuals is a forest. And forests are strong and they're beautiful and they work together and they feed other things and other things feed them.

"I like partying with people," he added, "you know, so, tonight I come and I get to see my friends, you know. And that's fun."

Fun that cost taxpayers more than one and half times the average Canadian's annual income for Georgie boy's night of fun.

CBC Covers For Layton

While Stephen Harper was called creepy, NDP leader Jack Layton was given a pass by CBC over a rather creepy incident – a visit to a massage parlour that ended in a police raid.

Just before the end of the election, *Toronto Sun* crime reporter Sam Pazzano broke the story of Layton being caught by police in a Dundas Street massage parlour naked.

Details recorded in a police officer's notebook from January 9, 1996, show that Layton was found lying on his back on a bed and was stark naked. He was in the company of a young, attractive Asian woman who police saw dispose of a wad of wet tissue.

The cop: "Did you receive any sexual services?"

The suspected john: "No sir, I was just getting a shiatsu."

The cop: "Why did you have all your clothes off?"

The suspected john: No answer.

The cop: "Are you aware that there were sex acts being done here?"

The suspected john: "No sir."

From the police notes.

Now despite being caught naked in a reputed bawdy house, Layton was given a free pass when the CBC finally got to ask him about the issue.

"Can I just ask you, when you went, police had suspicions about the place, did it look sketchy to you?" CBC reporter Rosemary Barton asked.

"Not at all," Layton said, "otherwise I wouldn't have gone in."

Not done with her tough line of questioning, Barton pushed on.

"Can I also just ask you how you reacted, cause I know you found out earlier in the day than we did that the report was coming out. Were you angry, were you upset, how did you react? Cause it's crazy that this came out two days before an election," Barton said.

And with that CBC had passed judgement on a story some of their own people had chased for years, declaring it a non-story because it attacked the wrong man.

Do you think for a minute that CBC would treat a story about Stephen Harper in a bawdy house just a little bit differently?

CBC Employees Make 39% More Than The Average Canadian

Documents released under access to information show that in 2007 full-time employees were earning an average of $55,712. The average income for Canadians in that time period was $40,092.

CBC: Journalist, Jury and Judge of Private Citizens

In March of 2010, CBC convicted a former crown prosecutor of sending innocent men to jail. George Dangerfield was a crown prosecutor for more than 30 years in Winnipeg dealing with hundreds of cases. CBC's "flagship" investigative journalism program reduced his career to just four cases and declared Dangerfield a crooked lawyer.

The fifth estate story focused on the case of Thomas Sophonow who was tried three times and convicted twice for the 1981 murder of Barbara Stoppel. His conviction was overturned and a public inquiry later cleared his name.

Dangerfield led the prosecution during Sophonow's first two trials. On the third trial Dangerfield doesn't even act as the crown attorney for the prosecution still CBC sets what will be a pattern – they blame Dangerfield for the entire mess.

Police, the Manitoba crown and two separate trials all found Sophonow guilty yet, to CBC, the blame lay with one man, George Dangerfield. *The fifth estate* would follow that pattern as they showcased three more cases.

Dangerfield, through his lawyer, had offered to sit down for an interview. It was an offer CBC reportedly declined. Another lawyer claimed to have been contacted by CBC about the show, but was never called back for an interview after he said positive things about Dangerfield.

While Dangerfield undoubtedly played a role in sending innocent men to jail, he was not alone. In the *Winnipeg Free Press*, Robert Marshall called the show "an unfair indictment of George Dangerfield."

Considering CBC's own record of false convictions and losses in court, perhaps they could have shown more balance with George Dangerfield.

CBC: Penny Wise and Pound Foolish

It is still the most iconic sports theme song in all of Canada, one that millions of us can hum on cue: The theme for *Hockey Night in Canada* played out over the CBC airwaves from 1968 until 2008. That's when CBC lost the song to CTV in a deal reportedly worth $2 - $3-million.

It didn't have to happen though.

While CTV clearly outbid CBC for the rights to use the song, the man who acted as the copyright agent for composer Dolores Claman has said CBC rejected a lowball offer. For years CBC had been paying Claman $500 for every broadcast game the song was used in. That same offer was on the table in 2008 but CBC rejected it.

"They did admit that the $500 per game was a fraction of what they spent on one net-cam," John Ciccone president of Copyright Music and Visuals told the *Toronto Sun*.

CBC opted to go their own way and paid well over a million dollars according to insiders to run a contest to find a new song. A song that is best described as completely forgettable.

CBC Is Great Because A Few CBC Fans Said So.

In November and December of 2011 a survey of "opinion leaders" was conducted for CBC by Phoenix Strategic Partners, a small polling firm in Ottawa. The state broadcaster had asked Phoenix to put together a panel of 2,000 "stakeholders" from across the country. These stakeholders were supposed to represent the broad swath of Canadian life.

In reality, CBC was paying Phoenix $56,000 to survey their friends and supporters. Of the 2,000 who were contacted, just 410 answered the questions.

Of the 410 élites surveyed, 80% said they had a favourable impression of the state broadcaster, while 70% agreed that CBC did a good job of "enriching democratic life."

A survey of employees was conducted at the same time but CBC refused to release those findings.

Voodo Economics CBC Style

In late 2011 CBC released a "study" conducted by the consulting firm Deloitte claiming that the annual

$1.1-billion tax dollars ploughed into CBC each year was worth $3.7-billion in economic spinoffs.

Let me say that again: CBC claimed that the $1.1-billion that you and I put into the state broadcaster each year resulted in an additional $3.7-billion worth of economic activity.

Michel Kelly-Gagnon, president of the Montreal Economic Institute, put it best when he asked "What kind of fools do they take us for?"

Apparently quite large fools and plenty of CBC supporters on Parliament Hill and in the media were willing to eat the study up.

But as Kelly-Gagnon pointed out, if investing in CBC gave the government that much of a return and an improvement in the economy, then they would be looking to put much more money into the state broadcaster.

"Indeed, if subsidizing the CBC produces such significant economic spin-offs, wouldn't the government have every reason to borrow money to create two or even three public broadcasters?"

Pipe down Michel, you don't want to give them any ideas.

CBC Absenteeism

In the summer of 2012, after years of stalling, CBC finally released the cost to taxpayers for employees who don't show up for work. According to documents prepared for CBC's own Board of Directors, the average number of sick days per CBC employee was 16.5 compared to just 12.6 days per employee in the wider public sector, and 8.9 days per employee in the private sector. The number one reason cited for both long term and short term absences was "mental disorders." CBC didn't have a solution to this problem but they did have a price tag: $17.7-million in fiscal year 2010-2011.

12

CBC Makes Broadcast History - Very Late

If you believed CBC's many fans, there would be no broadcasting in Canada without the "mother corp" as they call it. Of course that simply isn't true.

CBC didn't get started in Canada until 1936 whereas private broadcasting was underway in 1919.

The first radio station in Canada launched in Montreal on December 1, 1919 as XWA. A project of The Marconi Wireless Company, XWA would go on to become CFCF Radio, the first commercial broadcast station in the world. Other stations would pop up across Canada, including CKOC in Hamilton, Ontario in May 1922 and

CFNB in Fredricton, New Brunswick, begun in 1923. Also Vancouver had several competing stations by 1923, while Calgary had competition in the radio market as early as 1922.

By comparison CBC launched on November 2, 1936, almost a full 17 years after private radio began in Canada. The decision to launch CBC came after a Royal Commission in 1929 called for the establishment of a government owned, national broadcaster.

Just weeks after the report was delivered, the stock market crash of 1929 took the attention of Prime Minister Mackenzie King away from thoughts of starting a broadcaster. In 1930, two young socialists named Graham Spry and Alan Plaunt founded a lobby group called the Canadian Radio League to put pressure on the government of R.B. Bennett to launch a state broadcaster. Bennett eventually gave in.

When it came time for Canadians to get television, it was CBC that actually held back Canadian content. Broadcasting had been going on in limited fashion in the United States since 1939, and colour television was introduced by 1950, but CBC, which by this point was not only a radio network, but also the broadcast regulator for Canada, kept private innovation out of Canada.

When CBC launched television services in Canada in the fall of 1952, private stations were allowed, but only if they were CBC affiliates and carried CBC programming. This was one way CBC used its power as regulator to corner the market. Another method, long complained about by other broadcasters, was to ensure that CBC controlled all the best radio signals known as clear channels.

It took the courage of the Diefenbaker government in 1958 to strip away CBC's dual role as broadcaster and regulator to bring about real change in television. Shortly after the 1958 Broadcasting Act was passed new television stations were allowed in Canada and, within a few years, CTV was born.

Timeline of broadcasting in Canada	
Date	**Event**
December 1, 1919	XWA, later CFCF radio was launched
May 1, 1922	CKOC Hamilton
October 7, 1922	CFRC Kingston
1922-1927	Private radio stations pop up across Canada
1927	First national radio broadcast takes place marking the Diamond Jubilee of Confederation from Parliament Hill
1928	Canada's first national radio network, a partnership between private stations and Canadian National Railways, is launched
1929	Aird Commission established by Prime Minister McKenzie King recommends a government owned broadcaster
1936	CBC radio is launched
1952	CBC Television is launched Years after TV has been available in the United States and Britain

13

CBC Gets Dirty With Your Money

In December 2011, CBC victimized Canadians through a shady use of tax dollars once again. But rather than trying to hide the facts this time, CBC put them up on a website for all to see.

What had CBC done?

In an attempt to continue to be all things to all people and provide entertainment in whatever form Canadians wanted, CBC had purchased a porn program from France, and then posted it on one of their websites. The show never aired on CBC English or French, but it was freely available 24/7 on the French language website Tou.tv.

Yes, apparently someone at CBC decided that the internet didn't have enough pornography floating around on it, and what the world really needed was taxpayer funded porn.

The slogan for Tou.tv is *"de tout, quand vous le voulez"* which roughly translates as "everything, when you want it." Well now, if Canadians wanted pornography, they could get it on a government funded website, and know that the show had the taxpayers' seal of approval.

The story about CBC using taxpayers' dollars broke on *Byline*, my nightly television show on Sun News Network. Members of Parliament whose job it is to ensure tax dollars are properly spent were not too pleased. A reporter from the network had taken a number of raunchy scenes from the program and played them for MPs as they left their weekly caucus meetings.

"If this is the RDI using French actors through our tax system in order to produce this, I would say it is not a good use of taxpayers' dollars. I think most Canadians and Quebecers would say, 'What the heck is going on here?'," said Halifax area New Democrat, Peter Stoffer. "To allocate dollars for things of a sexual nature like this would make most Quebecers and most Canadians uncomfortable."

Lawrence MacAuley, a Liberal MP from Prince Edward Island agreed. "I can understand promoting the French language, but I certainly would not support anything that involves porn, that's for sure," said MacAuley.

Conservative MPs were equally unimpressed, or at least some of them. "I don't think my constituents would like paying for any television programming made outside of Canada. It doesn't look right to me," said Rob Merrifield, who represents an area that runs from the outskirts of

Edmonton to the Rockies, and includes Jasper National Park.

John Williamson, who headed up the Canadian Taxpayers Federation before entering politics, was also critical. "This kind of programming should not be on a broadcaster that is funded by taxpayers, that receives a billion dollars a year, this kind of industry does not need tax dollars to support it," Williamson said.

One man who was not critical initially was Heritage Minister James Moore. "I know you are in the business of going after the CBC, but I can't comment on something that I haven't seen," Moore said when asked about the program by reporter Kris Sims. Of course Moore could have seen the program, or at least excerpts loaded onto the iPad that Sims was carrying, but he refused to look.

Moore went further once the cameras and microphones were off.

In a very unusual move, especially for a senior cabinet minister, Moore stalked Sims to tell her that she was being used as a pawn by her Quebecor boss Pierre Karl Peladeau. Moore went on to claim that Peladeau was just trying to run down the CBC, and had hatched a plan to use an English all-news channel, Sun News, as a way to drive down CBC's ratings in French Quebec. When that happened Peladeau would shut down Sun News. None of this made sense of course but Moore was insistent.

"You know that's going to happen, right?" Moore said to Sims in the foyer of the House of Commons.

He then went on to compare pornography to the Sunshine girls that appear in Sun Media's tabloids. Moore, who was once accused of looking at porn on his laptop, should know the difference between porn and women in bikinis. In fact Moore's defence against the charge he was watching porn in the House of Commons – a charge leveled by New Democrat MP Irene Mathysen – was to say that he was showing someone photos of his girlfriend, which included some of her in a bikini.

What was doubly shocking is that Moore is not only the minister responsible for the CBC, he is also the point man on broadcasting regulations, magazine funds and so many other regulatory matters that touch on Quebecor business. Yet here was Moore, who holds enormous influence over all matters relating to media, defending tax dollars going to porn by attacking the integrity of a private sector CEO who put his own money on the line to build a Canadian media empire.

Sun Media newspapers ran an editorial calling for Moore to be fired. "James Moore's contempt for Quebecor's news operations is palpable, and can't be argued. In fact, he is so in love with the CBC that his knees figuratively weaken," the editorial read.

CBC defended the series.

"*Hard* is not considered a pornographic program. It is rated 16+," wrote Marco Dube, CBC's corporate spokesman. "Radio-Canada does not air pornographic series on any of its platforms."

CBC may not have considered their program to be pornographic, but it would have violated broadcasting codes to air scenes from the program unedited on Sun News. Even the images that did air during the network's coverage of the affair, complete with strategically placed CBC logos, generated complaints to Sun News that too much skin was being shown.

Images from the program showed full frontal nudity of men and women, scenes of orgies, scenes of pornography being made and sex scenes that were either real or very well simulated. All of these scenes were set amongst a plot line of a woman encountering the pornography industry for the first time.

Oh, the laughs that must ensue.

Defenders of the program and the state broadcaster attempted to argue that this was hardly hard core pornography and was, therefore, okay.

"This is all so silly I can hardly believe it," wrote Postmedia columnist Stephen Maher.

Maher, apparently also a porn aficionado, watched the show and declared it could not be considered pornographic. "If you actually watch a whole episode of *Hard*, as I have, you can't call it porn. It is more explicit than Sex and the City – because the French have a higher tolerance for such things than Americans do – but the ratio of sexy bits to non-sexy bit[s] is about the same," Maher wrote.

He then went on in the same conspiratorial tone as Moore had, declaring this all to be part of a plan to weaken CBC. Like many of the consensus media defenders of CBC, Maher claimed that since Videotron, a cable company owned by Quebecor, allowed subscribers to order porn channels, then everything was fine.

The distinction lost on Maher was the difference between public money, meaning tax dollars, and private money, meaning the dollars that come from owners or investors. If Quebecor or its subsidiaries wanted to invest in pornography, they could do so as long as investors were happy with that decision. CBC's investors consist of every taxpaying Canadian and, generally speaking, most Canadians don't view supplying pornography as a government service.

As for Quebecor being upset because of claims it was competition, a claim repeated often in the media, this simply wasn't true. Quebecor does not actually own any porn channels, its subsidiary Videotron simply offers them to those who wish to subscribe, as does just about every other cable company in North America.

While James Moore defended CBC's decision to use taxpayers' money to buy porn, that changed after his boss let his views be known. "While the government doesn't control CBC's content, we are confused by their decision to purchase sexually explicit content and make it available to children," said Andrew MacDougall, a spokesman for Prime Minister Stephen Harper. "The CBC's mandate is to deliver quality programming to the regions and rural areas, not this material."

Moore also issued a statement via email saying that he had watched the program and changed his views.

"Today I contacted the CBC and asked them to review all their online content to ensure offensive programming such as this is not repeated," Moore wrote.

CBC responded by changing the hours the program was available. Initially *Hard* was available to anyone who happened to stop by the government owned website, including children who stumbled upon it. CBC announced the change through their Facebook page. "Consistent with its policies and programs to ensure that the *Hard* series is not seen by children, Radio-Canada made the decision to limit the broadcast between midnight and 4 a.m. (EST)," the statement read.

Of course the change in hours didn't mean that taxpayers were no longer paying for porn, just that they were only paying for it to be seen between midnight and 4 a.m. – Montreal time. Any school kid in British

Columbia could still have access to this smut before bedtime while telling his mother he was only studying French on a CBC website.

CBC didn't apologize for buying the rights to the show, instead they pointed out that a show filled with sex was popular with young people. The idea that young people liked watching sex should not have been a surprise, and nor was it the point. The point was taxpayers were funding an inappropriate show. But CBC would stick with its defence for some time – young people like shows with sex.

About a week after the time change, CBC President Hubert Lacroix repeated the line that the show was popular with young people and defended keeping it. "This series is a web series that's been very successful in Europe. Also, it's a series that is in line with the mandate of tou.tv," Lacroix said following a speech to a business audience in Montreal.

While Lacroix and the rest of the gang at CBC defended the content of the program, they didn't like being personally attached to their very own show.

Sun News Network aired an edited clip that juxtaposed images from *Hard* against CBC vice-president Kirstine Stewart waxing poetic about how wonderful CBC was for Canada. The split screen video showed Stewart on one side talking about the state broadcaster while simulated sex from *Hard* was displayed on the other side.

The reaction from CBC was swift.

A lawyer's letter was sent to Sun Media demanding that the news outlet cease and desist in airing the clip. "Placing Ms. Stewart on the same screen as graphic sex scenes is indefensible morally and legally," wrote CBC lawyer Daniel Henry.

Another letter was sent, this one to Quebecor's board of directors, demanding that something be done to rein in Sun News. In his letter, Lacroix called the split screen with Stewart "an act so low and so unworthy that it must be drawn to your attention." The president of Canada's largest collection of broadcast journalists, who demands the government not interfere, and who defends CBC's own journalistic independence, even to the point of refusing to release costs, was now demanding that Quebecor's board interfere in newsroom operations.

Lacroix's hypocrisy was duly noted and his demands ignored.

CBC continued to defend their purchase of pornography using taxpayers' dollars until shortly before the 2012 federal budget, which was due at the end of March, and which promised tax cuts for every department. Against this backdrop, and against the charge that spending tax dollars on smut showed the state broadcaster had too much money, the show was quietly dropped.

"This show is no longer available on Tou.tv," said a notice that appeared on the series' page on March 8, 2012. "Visit our site regularly to know when the show might resume."

But CBC had no plans of bringing the show back.

"We prefer offering series that are available around the clock," spokesman March Pichette told the newspaper *Le Devoir.*

14

CBC Shoots The Messenger

When CBC was brought under the access to information system in September 2007, it should have heralded a new era of openness at the state broadcaster. Canadians who had long watched their tax dollars go to a broadcaster that didn't represent them, and worse yet, held much of the country in disdain, could now hope to find out exactly what those tax dollars were paying for.

Of course we now know that it didn't work out that way.

From an overzealous use of their exemption on journalistic or programming matters, to claims that releasing information would be detrimental to the economic interests of Canada, CBC knew how to keep their secrets secret.

Of course in those early days their favourite way to keep Canadians in the dark was simply to refuse to release any information. Under the law, any request that does not get a response within 30 days is deemed to have been refused. A response can be anything from actually releasing the material to asking for more time, but in hundreds of its early cases CBC did neither. In fact they wouldn't even acknowledge the refusals.

This pattern earned them bad reports from the Information Commissioner's Office, but didn't really cause any headaches. Most media wouldn't touch a negative story about the CBC, and politicians were generally afraid to poke the beast lest they be the subject of negative stories themselves.

Sure CBC had to put up with the odd *Sun* story about lavish expenses on hotels and booze, but since the other media outlets didn't follow-up and join in questioning why tax dollars were being wasted, the state broadcaster could laugh it off and continue with business as usual.

That changed in November 2010.

I began writing a new feature that appeared in Sun Media newspapers across Canada. Called *The Money Drain*, the feature consisted of a regular report of all the things CBC wasn't telling the public. Stories about their refusal to release a list of cars, the cost of absenteeism or their fight with the information commissioner over the cost of replacing the *Hockey Night in Canada* theme song began appearing several times a week.

The stories themselves were not long, but followed a formula normally well-loved by members of the Ottawa press pack: File an access to information request and then report on what the government refused to release to the public. The implication always is that the government is hiding something if they hold back some documents or remove much of the material.

In the case of CBC, they were hiding plenty.

There were three years' worth of access to information requests, most of which resulted in little to no information released even when the bureaucrats at CBC finally got around to responding at all. *The Money Drain* series used a tactic often employed by CBC against the government only this time it was CBC that was the target. They didn't like it.

Within a few days of detailing CBC's problems with openness and transparency, the state broadcaster responded with a series of pricey newspaper ads that promised Canadians they would be up front with information.

They ran ads that boasted of tens of thousands of pages released under Access to Information, but failed to mention that tens of thousands of pages had also been released with all relevant information removed, the result being either blank pages or pages covered in black marker.

"Transparency and accountability are core values that have always guided, and will continue to guide, the way we manage public funds," CBC President Hubert Lacroix crowed in a news release that announced the ads.

CBC was using taxpayer's money to build a war room capacity so they could fight back against claims that they were misusing taxpayer dollars, or were keeping Canadians in the dark. Eventually, what came to light was that they were again misusing taxpayer dollars and continuing to keep Canadians in the dark.

In addition to running expensive ads, CBC began to take the threat of Quebecor seriously. If their rival was successful in exposing mismanagement of money, then the party could be over. Executives at CBC began building a briefing book on how to respond to Quebecor.

Obtaining documents about the discussions that led to the placement of newspaper ads trumpeting a new era of openness should have been an easy task, but that would be in a normal government operation, not from CBC. In the midst of the 2011 bombing campaign in Libya, where Canadian soldiers and airmen were putting their lives on the line to help oust Muammar Gadhafi, CBC was able to report on briefing notes about the mission provided to Foreign Affairs Minister John Baird. You would think that if a media outlet could find out about an ongoing military operation through access to information, then finding out about the state broadcaster would be simple. Not so.

Getting notes on CBC buying newspaper ads to promote how open they were being would prove more difficult; some of the documents were destroyed.

In one e-mail Peter Hull, the man in charge of the access to information system at CBC, said that he had slipped his comments under the door of communications manager Marco Dube.

A request to see those notes was turned down – not because they couldn't be released, but because the CBC said it could not find them. It appears Dube destroyed the notes deeming them a "transitory record."

After the ads appeared and Lacroix's news release announced the new era, CBC went back to its old ways of declining to provide information to the public, and whining about their heavy burden.

"CBC/Radio-Canada is the only journalistic enterprise in the country subject to Access to Information," Bill Chambers, CBC's vice-president of communications wrote in a posting to CBC's website.

CBC of course is also the only journalistic enterprise in the country that gets more than $1-billion per year from the taxpayer. Taking $100-million dollars every 30 days from taxpayers didn't seem to be a sufficient reason to Chambers and the rest at CBC for cultivating a commitment to financial accountability.

That same missive from Chambers went on to attack Quebecor for daring to ask questions. Chambers accused Quebecor of being "zealous" in its use of the access to information system to find out how CBC spends taxpayers' money.

A day after the Chambers rant was posted, CBC took the highly unusual step of publishing an English translation of an opinion piece that had originally appeared in the separatist newspaper *Le Devoir*. The column was written by Marc-Francois Bernier, a University of Ottawa professor who used the words of a locked out worker to malign Quebecor.

Writing on a meeting of the Federation of Professional Journalists of Quebec, a group well at odds with Quebecor, a major employer of journalists, Bernier cited complaints by journalists who had been locked out just ahead of their threatened strike. The lockout had been ongoing for 2 years at this point. Still, Bernier acted as stenographer for the complaints.

"During a workshop last Saturday on the extent of Quebecor Media's influence, David Patry, a journalist with the *Journal de Montréal* who has been locked out for nearly two years, denounced the fact that he had been encouraged and even required to write and sign articles attacking Radio-Canada as well as a journalist from the daily newspaper *La Presse*," Bernier wrote.

CBC took an op-ed published in a newspaper that competes with Quebecor, that used the words of locked out workers complaining about the company and treated it as fact, even publishing it on their own website. Now CBC was using tax dollars to strike back at those who dared to question their entitlements.

Things would turn nastier a little while later when the state broadcaster would turn to outright fabrication to turn the channel away from their ongoing resistance to openness.

In October 2011, CBC released a "Get the Facts" document that was short on facts. Titled, "What Quebecor won't tell you about its attacks on the public broadcaster," the document claimed that Quebecor received more than $500-million in subsidies over the prior three years.

The document, as well as talking points and a six-page attack on Quebecor, were distributed to all Members of Parliament.

To arrive at the claim that Quebecor took half a billion dollars in subsidies, CBC added up all government programs for TV and magazines, and then invented a new subsidy for cell phone service. According to CBC, Quebecor had received a $333 million subsidy when the Government of Canada had auctioned off spectrum rights for new entries into the mobile phone market.

In an attempt to encourage competition in the mobile phone market the government had set aside a certain amount of wireless spectrum for new entrants. Quebecor's Videotron bid and won part of that spectrum auction. According to CBC this process amounted to a subsidy. The truth is that Quebecor had argued for a free-market solution that would have included allowing the company to raise capital in foreign markets to compete with Bell and Rogers. The government declined to lift foreign ownership restrictions and set the rules of the auction. The auction that took place saw Quebecor pay the government $540-million for the right to start a new mobile phone company, in CBC's world this is a subsidy.

CBC also pointed to $13-million paid over three years through the Canadian Periodical fund, a fund used by virtually every magazine published in Canada.

CBC was correct to point out that Quebecor's television stations took in $192-million over three years from various funds, but what they didn't tell the public was that CBC snapped up about $277-million over the same period.

So, over the three years from 2008 to 2010, CBC had taken in roughly $3.3-billion in direct taxpayer subsidy, and they could draw some kind of equivalency with Quebecor, or expose hypocrisy by the latter, because, over the same period of time, they took in approximately $205-million taxpayer dollars!

Another annoying detail that CBC failed to discuss is that Quebecor had gone on the record several times calling for the elimination of these special funds. CBC, on the other hand, has vigorously defended them.

Of course CBC didn't just set its sights on Quebecor or Sun Media as a whole; they also targeted specific journalists – myself and Ezra Levant.

I had kicked off the *Money Drain* series for the Sun Media papers and exposed the state broadcaster as a laggard when it came to being upfront and honest with the public. On our daily programs on the Sun News

Network, both Ezra and I kept a close and critical eye on CBC.

After Levant paid a visit to CBC's Toronto headquarters in August 2011 to shoot part of his show and ask for an interview with Lacroix, someone filed an access request looking for documents on what had happened the day that Levant got booted from the CBC building. Prior to releasing the information, CBC sent Levant a copy of the documents and asked him what confidential information he was willing to waive for release. The answer was all of it.

Levant went on air with the documents to reveal that, as CBC executives exchanged emails on how to deal with his visit to their building, some outrageous proposals were proposed. One executive actually suggested sending the crew from the comedy show *This Hour Has 22 Minutes* to launch a "counter attack" on Levant. Meanwhile CBC's vice-president, Kirstine Stewart, suggested the state broadcaster hire him.

The CBC way: If you can't refute your critics, pay them to shut up.

My own record was long but shrouded in secrecy. CBC amassed 547 pages on me between June 2010 and early 2012. After the experience of Levant revealing all, CBC decided not to risk sending me any documents in advance for clearance. Most were simply redacted (edited to remove much of the information).

Sending the team from This Hour has 22 Minutes out as a political attack team isn't really that far-fetched. In late October 2011, Toronto Mayor Rob Ford was accosted in his own driveway as he tried to leave for work early in the morning.

After Ford began walking from his front door to his

driveway, CBC's Mary Walsh, AKA Marg Delahunty, ran screaming towards him dressed in her "warrior princess" costume and with a camera at her side. Walsh was shouting at Ford saying that she came up from Newfoundland to give him advice. Ford kept politely asking her to let him get in his car. Frustrated Ford went back inside.

"One good thing about being stubborn Mayor Ford is that you always know what you're going to be thinking the next day," Walsh yelled at Ford as he tried to make his way back into his home.

Yes because only enlightened CBC liberals like Wash have open minds.

Just like Richard Nixon, CBC keeps an enemies list and they are not above using taxpayers' money to strike out at those who dare to question them.

15

CBC Takes Aim At Gun Owners

When CBC reporters have you in their cross hairs, be wary.

Despite claims that reporters at the state broadcaster are neutral, objective individuals only interested in pursuing the truth, the CBC has an agenda and it pushes it hard. Just ask any political group on the wrong side of the downtown Toronto group thinking that dominates CBC's newsrooms.

In September 2010, just ahead of a vote on scrapping the long-gun registry, CBC turned its sights on Canadian gun advocates and let loose a flurry of misinformation, lies and spin.

Candice Hoeppner, a Conservative MP from Portage-Lisgar in Manitoba, had introduced a private members bill, Bill C-391, to scrap the long-gun registry, in 2009. The gun registry came about as a Liberal promise of the Chrétien government in the 1990s.

Originally promised as a way to curb gun violence and shootings like the massacre at *Ecole Polytechinque* in 1989, the gun registry never delivered. Firstly instead of targeting criminals and gangs, it targeted law abiding gun owners – farmers, hunters and sport shooters. It made the simple possession of a gun a crime unless the owner had the proper licence exempting them from what had now become a criminal activity. The bill that brought about the gun registry, Bill C-68, also changed Canadian law in fundamental ways, it allowed warrantless searches and the seizure of private property without compensation. It also delegated authority to reclassify firearms as banned to the RCMP without Parliamentary oversight.

Those who claimed the gun registry bill was the first step towards a police state were not overstating their case, unlike most supporters they had actually read the bill and could see what was coming.

Then there was the cost.

Then Justice Minister Allan Rock had promised that the cost to taxpayers to register all legal firearms in Canada and make the country safer from people like Marc Lepine would cost no more than $2-million. In the end the cost was closer to $2-billion and still the registry didn't work.

The Conservative Party, as well as the Canadian Alliance and Reform Party before it, had promised to end the gun registry, and the unfair treatment law abiding gun owners had faced under the new regime. As

Stephen Harper formed his first Conservative minority government in early 2006, Auditor General Sheila Fraser was finishing up a report on the gun registry program that should have had everyone questioning its worth. But not the CBC.

Fraser found that the gun registry program had regularly misreported its costs to Parliament by tens of millions of dollars per year. Then there was the question of the shoddy data. Much of what was recorded in the gun registry database was inaccurate, according to the audit report.

Rational people are expected to follow the wisdom often attributed to left-wing economist John Maynard Keynes, who apparently said, "When I find new information I change my mind; What do you do?" Not CBC. In this case, it answered Keynes' question by doubling down with its support for the long gun registry.

So on September 13, 2010, a week before the vote on Hoeppner's bill, CBC's flagship newscast *The National* presented a story that would have unsuspecting Canadians believing that it was an American group – The National Rifle Association – that was behind the legislation and all the lobbying to repeal the $2-billion boondoggle known as the gun registry.

"The debate over Canada's gun registry has been highly political in advance of next week's Parliamentary vote and it's been highly divisive," anchor Peter Mansbridge intoned in his most serious voice. "But if you think it only involves Canadians, you would be wrong. A powerful American lobby group has found its way into this."

That was Mansbridge's introduction to a lopsided, biased and inaccurate report by, as he described her,

CBC's senior investigative correspondent. Diana Swain then took over and tipped her hand by the way she described the NRA.

"Peter, The National Rifle Association, or The NRA, might be the most influential and controversial lobby group in the United States," Swain told the audience.

Powerful yes. The NRA is undoubtedly a powerful lobby group thanks to its more than 4 million members and their advocacy for the second amendment to the U.S. constitution which guarantees the right of every American to bear arms. But, while the NRA is controversial to the CBC and people like Swain, it counts Americans from across the political spectrum as members. Even liberal Democrat Howard Dean, the former governor of Vermont and head of the Democratic National Committee was able to obtain a full endorsement from the NRA.

None of that mattered to CBC, the point of their story was to scare Canadians that big bad gun loving Americans were set to invade and impose their gun laws on the True North Strong and Free. Swain claimed that the NRA sees part of its mandate as fighting gun control laws around the world. What she didn't say is that the NRA's constitution forbids spending money on Canadian or any other international lobbying.

Swain's hit job on opponents of the gun registry could easily have led Canadians to believe that the NRA was active in Canada when in fact it was never even interested. Part of the television story featured footage from a documentary produced by the NRA for an American TV audience about the Canadian gun registry experience. The project cost $100,000 and aired on an American TV network. Swain presented this as if it were an investment in the Canadian anti-gun registry movement.

As for further evidence of the NRA being involved in Canadian politics, Swain points to a speech given to a Canadian Shooting Sports Association dinner by a former NRA president, and a claim by CSSA president Tony Bernardo that the NRA has given him "tremendous amounts of logistical support" in his campaign against the gun registry.

Advice in Swain's world counts as activism.

The claim that the NRA was highly involved in the fight against the gun registry in Canada is of course a false one. If the same standard were applied to CBC, then it could be claimed that the BBC or American media companies, which CBC consults, control – or run – parts of Canada's state broadcaster. Of course that claim would be ludicrous.

To help her story, Swain turned to a retired and disgraced Liberal politician, former Ontario Attorney General Michael Bryant who, without presenting any proof, claimed that he's been aware of NRA lobbying in Canada since 1999. At this point in the story, he and Swain tip their hand on why this story is being run: It is meant to scare Canadians.

"For a lot of people in Canada, if they knew that the NRA was part of the effort to get rid of the gun registry, they would think more about their views," Bryant said. "And they would think, 'well, wait a minute, I thought this was about, you know, wasting taxpayer dollars. The NRA's involved? Really? That makes me very uncomfortable.'"

Facts didn't seem to have any impact on Bryant's views. The former Liberal politician had been Ontario's Attorney General during Toronto's Summer of the Gun. In 2005, there were 52 homicides with guns in Toronto, with 16 shooting deaths occurring in the time period from the Victoria Day long weekend until Labour Day. These shootings were not stopped by the long gun registry; the murders were not solved with the long gun registry. None of his gun control advocacy has stopped the problem of illegal handguns used by crooks and gangsters on Toronto's streets.

In spite of those facts, Bryant was willing to go on CBC and malign law abiding owners of rifles and shotguns as dangerous and unCanadian. Even worse, the state broadcaster was willing to let him do that, even giving him a prominent place in their story.

The other man with a prominent place in the story, Tony Bernardo with the Canadian Shooting Sports Association, was not afforded the same courtesy.

CBC pieced together their made-up story of Americans infiltrating Canada's gun debate without interviewing Bernardo on camera. They said he was out of country. Most media outlets would have waited until they could speak to a main player in their story; not CBC.

With a vote looming to kill or save the gun registry, CBC could waste no time in scaring the public about the evils of the American hordes waiting to invade with their pro-gun ways. If enough members of the public were scared, that might place pressure on the Liberal and NDP Members of Parliament who had won their northern and rural seats by promising to scrap the gun registry.

While often portrayed by Toronto media elites like those at CBC as a partisan issue, the desire to end the gun registry went across party lines in many parts of the country, especially outside of the biggest cities like Montreal, Toronto and Vancouver. CBC's ploy worked, and in the end enough opposition MPs who had promised to end the gun registry flipped their votes and did the opposite of what they had promised their voters.

It would take another election and a majority government to rid Canada of the gun registry.

16

When In Doubt, Blame Israel

Just how bad is CBC's reporting on Israel?

In the week before Christmas 2011, Ginette Lamarche, a radio reporter for CBC's French language service, actually used the term *naqba* during a conversation with a radio host. The term *naqba* is used by Palestinians to describe the creation of Israel, naqba means catastrophe.

"There have been at the *naqba*, that is to say the arrival of Israel in 1948..." Lamarche said, going on to describe large protests populated by young people. What she didn't tell her audience is that *naqba* is a loaded political statement that delegitimizes Israel.

This incident is hardly the only time CBC's French language reporter has expressed an anti-Israel bias in her reporting. She has been upbraided by the ombudsman on more than one occasion. In fact on February 14, 2012, Lamarche was cited in a report that reviewed five of her stories in the lead-up to Christmas 2011. It was found that all five failed to meet the "the values of accuracy, balance and impartiality of Journalistic Standards and Practices of CBC."

Ombudsman Pierre Tourangeau critiqued Lamarche for only putting forward Palestinian viewpoints in her reporting during this period, and not offering any dissenting voices whether Israeli or otherwise. "On a few occasions, she has taken over the claims of those she interviewed. For these reasons, these reports have at least an appearance of bias," Tourangeau wrote.

The response from CBC management was swift – silence.

Eric Duhaime, a Quebec political commentator and columnist for *Journal de Montreal* and Sun Media, took CBC to task for their refusal to deal with such blatant bias.

"Diffusing information about the most publicized conflict in the world is not an easy task," Duhaime wrote almost two weeks after the ombudsman's report. "Unfortunately, there are practically no other French Canadians who have the privilege of being paid to live there and report on what's going on in that hot region. When the leftist biases are expressed daily on the Crown Corporation's airwaves on national issues, there is at least a counterweight in other media to allow listeners to hear both sides and form their own opinions. This is not the case in French Canada with news from Tel Aviv or Jerusalem."

Unfortunately CBC's bias against Israel isn't confined to broadcasts in French; the English network has plenty to offer as well.

CBC's Neil Macdonald was the chief Middle East correspondent for the state broadcaster from 1998 until 2003. His time in the region was marked with what many saw as a strong anti-Israel tone. CanWest newspapers, *National Post* in particular, heavily criticized Macdonald's reporting. When company executive Leonard Asper called Macdonald out publicly, the reporter demanded an apology.

None was forthcoming.

During his time in the Middle East Macdonald refused to use the word terrorist, even for those who blew up restaurants filled with civilians.

"Everybody's a friggin' terrorist!" Macdonald told the Ryerson Review of Journalism in 2005. "The word has lost all meaning. It has been misused so often."

Yet even groups on the Government of Canada's official terrorist watch list would not receive the designation from Macdonald. Hamas, which stands for *Harakat Al-Muqawama Al-Islamiya*, or Islamic Resistance Movement, was added to Canada's list of terrorist groups in 2002, as was Hezbollah, yet neither of them have ever been called terrorists by Macdonald.

While Macdonald avoided the word terrorist, he didn't mind invoking the term war crimes when talking about Israel in a 2004 online op-ed published on the CBC website. "The Israeli soldiers who enforce the occupation kill a great many Palestinian civilians. If the Palestinians have committed terrorism, so the argument goes, the Israelis have certainly committed war crimes. There is also the question of whether the Jewish settlers in the West Bank and Gaza, thousands of whom are well armed and overtly bellicose, constitute civilians or combatants."

Terrorist is actually a word that CBC has a policy of not using, unless it is said by someone else. "It is the CBC's practice – and it has been the practice in CBC newsrooms for over 30 years now – to try to avoid using the words 'terror' and 'terrorist' on their own as a form of description without attribution," Esther Enkin, executive editor of CBC News wrote in response to a complaint in 2011.

Of course some groups have still been called terrorist groups on the state broadcaster, just ask the Jewish Defence League of Canada.

In a segment on the Anders Brevik shooting in Norway that took place in the summer of 2011, CBC's in-house terrorism expert called the JDL a terrorist group. "There are extremists in every religion," he said, "whether it's Islam, whether it's Christianity, whether it's Hinduism, even Buddhists. The Jewish Defence League is a banned terrorist organization in Canada."

Complaints poured in and Enkin was forced to deal with the issue. "It is not [a terrorist organization], of course," Enkin wrote, "Although the Jewish Defence League is identified as a terrorist organization by the United States government. CBC News security specialist Bill Gillespie intended to refer to *Kahane Chai* (or Kach), which is on the Canadian government list of terrorist organizations, and not the JDL."

If using the word terrorist to describe Jewish groups while refusing to use it for Hamas or Hezbollah does not show a bias at CBC, nothing will.

Critics of the reporter and CBC's coverage of Israel in general, such as Honest Reporting Canada, were relieved when Macdonald was reassigned from Jerusalem to Washington in 2004, but that hasn't stopped the reporter from working negative references to Israel into his stories.

In May 2004, Macdonald filed a report on the Abu Ghraib prisoner abuse scandal. The scandal had come to light through self-reporting by the US military. Soldiers were suspended, some were charged and prosecuted. The military had informed the media about the abuse in early 2004, but there was little reporting of the issue at first. By spring there was a media frenzy surrounding the issue.

It was in this time period that Macdonald interviewed Eugene Bird of the Council on the National Interest. Bird asserted that Israeli intelligence was involved in the abuse at Abu Ghraib. There was no supporting evidence for the claim, nor was Bird identified as a pro-Palestinian activist. Macdonald's defence? Ignorance!

"Had I known Eugene Bird was also fronting a pro-Palestinian group, I would have said so," Macdonald told Ryerson.

The report resulted in two on-air apologies.

Bird was not the only "expert" with a strong anti-Israel streak that Macdonald would profile from his perch in Washington. Michael Sheuer, a former CIA officer told Macdonald in a one-on-one interview that American support for Israel was costing American lives. "Right now the perception in the Muslim world and in much of the world I would think is that the Israeli tail is leading the American dog. And that costs the United States," Sheuer told Macdonald.

In his follow-up question Macdonald blamed Israel for the creation of Osama bin Laden. "You know it is political heresy in Washington to draw a direct line between Osama bin Laden and Israel or Osama bin Laden and America's, the United States of America's policies in the Middle East," Macdonald stated.

Sheuer responded, "As long as that's heresy more Americans are going to die."

Despite his credentials as a former CIA member, Sheuer has expressed strong anti-Israeli views. This is a man who would later describe both the Republicans and the Democrats as "wholly owned subsidiaries of the American Israeli Public Affairs Committee (AIPAC) and the Israeli government."

On February 14, 2011, Macdonald, the Washington correspondent, was reporting on the Middle East once again. This time he was covering the Arab spring, still then in its infancy, but old enough to have brought about strong reactions from local governments trying to hang onto power.

In a story about brutal regimes using rubber bullets, tear gas and emergency laws to stay in power, Macdonald found a way to work in a reference to Israel being just as bad.

"Repressive emergency laws are used extensively throughout the Middle East," Macdonald told his audience. "President Barack Obama repeatedly denounced Egypt's during the protests. The trouble is most Arabs know that Israel has an emergency law too which it uses for such things as detention without trial and confiscation or demolition of Palestinian property."

This wasn't the first time Macdonald used this tactic and it wouldn't be the last.

In an April 2011 story about the fight for Ajdabiya, Libya, Macdonald was reporting on how brutal Muammar Gadhafi's fighters had been to the few locals who had now fled town. He included a clip of a man, Macdonald doing the translation himself.

"Salusi Saad Izwi holds up the bloody robe of his uncle Suleiman Bulaj. 'Does this look like a military uniform,' he asks? His uncle was the caretaker of a local mosque and was shot down in his own yard. 'Gadhafi is like the Israelis,' says Izwi, summoning the worst insult he can manage, 'he kills whomever he likes.'"

Of course the story had nothing to do with Israel, and Macdonald surely could have found other locals who had harsh words for Gadhafi without mentioning Israel. Instead he chose to insert the clip and, by extension, insert Israel, into a story about rebels trying to overthrow the Mad Dog of Tripoli.

Macdonald is not alone at the CBC in being critiqued for having a bias in favour of the Palestinians, he's just the lightning rod.

In a report on the second attempt by left-wing activists to hire ships for a run at the naval blockade of Gaza, CBC reporter Alexandra Szacka sounded more like a cheerleader than a reporter when she filed on a behind-the-scenes look at the Canadian ship in the second flotilla.

"This might look like a group of people preparing for an adventure but instead they are about to embark on a dangerous mission," Szacka told viewers at the opening of her report.

Her report then went on to showcase the inside of the Tahrir, the name given the boat in honour of the central point of Egypt's protest movement. She detailed the

145

harsh conditions its nearly 50 passengers would face on a planned three-day journey across the Mediterranean, but she did not air a single response to any tough question about their agenda, assuming any were asked.

The report never explained the context of the blockade, nor offered any dissenting opinion. In fact, with the use of terms like Freedom Flotilla, the entire piece could have been written and produced by pro-Palestinian activists.

CBC has a soft spot for Palestinian activists, including those who have broken international sanctions like British MP George Galloway. Galloway, a one-time Labour MP booted from the party by Tony Blair for being too radical, has toured the world promoting the Palestinian cause. In 2009, he even organized an aid convoy for Gaza that got him in hot water with Canadian authorities. The incident, however, turned him into a star for the CBC crowd.

In February 2006, the terrorist group Hamas won elections in the Gaza Strip. Governments around the world, including the Canadian government, refused to deal with Hamas, instead, imposing sanctions. Hamas had been responsible for more than a decade of attacks on Israel ranging from suicide bombs to rocket attacks, and had long held that Israel should cease to exist.

Galloway was no stranger to fighting sanctions imposed on Muslim countries. In 1994, as Iraq dealt with sanctions following the first Gulf War, Galloway met with Saddam Hussein and told the brutal leader, "Sir, I salute your courage, your strength, your indefatigability." Despite having said the words in English and on camera, Galloway would claim his words were taken out of context.

The words he spoke on March 10, 2009, could hardly be taken out of context by CBC but, to protect Galloway's reputation, they could be ignored. Galloway arrived in Gaza with his aid convoy on that day, and in front of television cameras and a large crowd, announced that he was breaking international sanctions and giving cash to Hamas.

"Just in case the British government or the European Union want to face me in any court, let me tell them live on television, I personally am about to break the sanctions on the elected government of Palestine," Galloway told cheering crowds. "We make no apology for what I am about to say. We are giving them to the elected government of Palestine, to the prime minister, Ismail Haniya, here is the money," Galloway said. Holding a bag up and handing it to Haniya, Galloway declared, "This is not charity, this is politics."

Agence France Presse and other news agencies present reported that Galloway's cash gift to the Hamas government was 25,000 British pounds.

Scheduled for a visit to Canada on a speaking tour a month later, Galloway was informed that his actions may prevent him from entering Canada. He was never banned despite claims to the contrary. He never tried to enter the country. In an interview with CBC's "flagship" program *The Hour* with George Stroumboulopoulos, the issue of the money being handed over to Hamas never came up. Instead the alleged "ban" on Galloway was presented as a freedom of speech issue.

Suddenly CBC, which had not rushed to the defence of domestic freedom fighters Mark Steyn or Ezra Levant when they were facing prosecution before human rights bodies in Canada, became champions of free speech for George Galloway.

Despite finding footage of Galloway praising Hussein in Iraq 15 years earlier, and his appearance on Britain's celebrity big brother purring like a cat, CBC could not find the readily available footage or quotes of Galloway saying he was giving money to a terrorist group that had repeatedly attacked Israel. Galloway made the unchallenged statement that he was "banned" from Canada and was branded a terrorist for delivering humanitarian aid to Gaza. "Twenty-four ambulances, a fire engine, trucks full of wheel chairs, children's nappies, biscuits, food, medicines, it's an odd definition of terrorism, no?" Galloway put to Stroumboulopoulos.

It would be an odd-definition of terrorism if it were true. Unfortunately, if you rely on CBC for your news you wouldn't know any better.

Stroumboulopoulos didn't challenge Galloway's statement; nor did he show his audience the readily available video images of Galloway handing money over to a terrorist group and challenging the authorities to arrest him for breaking the law.

CBC's first instinct is to blame Israel – then offer an apology and correction if they are caught.

17

CBC Hates Conservatives

If there was one word that had to be chosen to sum up the general attitude CBC has to conservative minded Canadians it would be hostility.

CBC, as its former head of English services Richard Stursberg put it, is "...soft left, anti-business, Toronto-centric, politically correct..." To the CBC, conservative minded Canadians and the Conservative Party are the enemy.

Sometimes this has played out in subtle ways such as what CBC chooses to cover and what to ignore. Talk to anyone involved in the pro-life movement and they will have instant stories of indifference expressed by

CBC news personnel in their stories and their cause. In the news judgment of CBC, a small protest railing against the Conservative government and the robocall controversy is deserving of extensive coverage across all platforms while the annual March for Life, which draws 15,000 to protest abortion, warrants minimal coverage.

Author and broadcaster Michael Coren, currently host of *The Arena* on Sun News Network, actually worked for the CBC once upon a time as a writer. Since then he has appeared on numerous shows as a commentator. Coren has published 14 bestselling books and been a national affairs columnist for several daily newspapers for more than 10 years. Yet, despite all this, Coren noted that the calls from CBC to appear on their programs began to dry up until one day he was told to his face that his views were no longer welcomed.

"I was asked to appear on a show on CBC *Newsworld* to discuss political leadership qualities," Coren said. "I was pre-interviewed, booked, confirmed. I arrived at reception to be told, 'there's a problem.' I was then passed by phone to a producer who told me, 'I'm really sorry, but the union here didn't like a column you wrote last week. We can't have you on.'"

Coren protested, but to no avail, he described the woman telling him he was cancelled as seeming "intimidated and under pressure." He wrote about the experience in a newspaper column and was denounced by the head of *Newsworld* who wrote a letter to the editor in reply. The entire affair was denied even though no checks had been done to see if the story Coren was telling was true.

"It's not unique, and I – just one person – have several similar and even worse stories," Coren said.

Simply put, Coren was a conservative minded Canadian who actually believed the things he said instead of showing up on TV to agree with liberals, as so many of the favoured conservatives did. Coren was a victim of CBC's subtle hostility to conservative ideas.

Other times, CBC has been openly hostile to conservative thought and conservative principles.

In mid-November 2000, as the federal election was entering into its final leg, CBC ran an in-depth piece on Canadian Alliance leader Stockwell Day. Day had won the leadership of the party the previous summer and was riding a wave of positive press and momentum. Then came the "special" report from the state broadcaster.

Called *"Fundamental Day,"* the mini-documentary looked at Stockwell Day's religious beliefs and, through the lens of reporter Paul Hunter, those beliefs appeared frightening. In his book, *War Room*, Liberal strategist Warren Kinsella called the report "a gift."

"On the evening of Tuesday, November 14, 2000, with just under two weeks to go in the Canadian federal election campaign, the clouds parted, an angelic chorus sang and a gift descended from the heavens," Kinsella wrote.

Why was this report a gift from heaven? Because it played up stereotypes and asked questions about Day's religious faith that would not be asked of any other leader in that election campaign.

Was Day a new-earth creationist? Did he believe Adam and Eve were real people? Did he believe that man was fallen due to the sins of Adam and Eve? What did his faith teach about homosexuality?

All of these questions were posed and answered, plus more, during Paul Hunter's report for CBC's *The National*. Day was portrayed as someone who believed that the earth was less than 10,000 years-old, who believed Adam and Eve were real, that they had sinned and thus been banished from the Garden of Eden. He was even portrayed as someone who didn't think homosexuality should be taught in sex-ed classes, and that gay adoption should not be allowed.

It didn't matter that all of Day's views were held by a significant portion of the Canadian public. It didn't matter that many Jews and Muslims also believe that the earth is less than 10,000 years-old or that the Catholic faith of Chrétien teaches all the other views. It didn't matter because showing context wasn't the point of the report; scaring the Canadian public away from the scary fundamentalist was.

Hunter was also able to find someone who said that Day believed humans walked with dinosaurs. His fate was sealed. The media, led by the CBC, mocked Day incessantly. Stories about his faith piled up while other leaders were given a free ride.

This wouldn't be the last time that CBC used election coverage to attempt to stop a conservative politician from taking power.

In the 2011 election that saw Stephen Harper win his majority government, the difference in tone between the questions asked of Harper and those asked of his opponents was remarkable.

Early in the campaign, a story appeared in the *London Free Press* about a woman who claimed she was turfed from a Conservative event featuring Harper. The woman, Awish Aslam, told the *Free Press* that she had been ejected from an event she had pre-registered to attend because of a Facebook photo of her meeting Liberal leader Michael Ignatieff a week earlier. The consensus media picked up on the story and ran with it, pestering Harper about restrictions on meeting real Canadians for the rest of the campaign.

That same *Free Press* story also told of two reporters from the paper being roughed up at an Ignatieff event. One of the reporters told the Mounties assigned to guard Ignatieff to be careful, that she was pregnant.

"That's what you get for rushing a bodyguard," the Mountie reportedly said.

No one asked Ignatieff to defend the two journalists being roughed up by his security detail, but Harper was dogged about volunteers barring a woman from an event. Both were relevant lines of questioning but only one was followed.

"It's about a question you've been asked before about your insistence on campaigning inside a protective bubble," CBC's top political reporter Terry Milewski asked Harper in Victoriaville, QC. "Your campaign seems determined to confirm this impression sometimes in quite creepy ways by kicking out of your campaign events voters who haven't been pre-screened or loyalty tested by your campaign. You've had most famously a student kicked out because of the crime of having a picture of Michael Ignatieff on her Facebook page which a lot of Canadians find to be kind of creepy."

Milewski wasn't done yet and went on to accuse Harper of being undemocratic, contrary to Canadian tradition – and creepy once more before letting the prime minister speak in response.

Talk about creepy.

In fact no other political leader in the 2011 election campaign faced questions as hostile as that from any media outlet.

Of course the 2011 election was hardly the first time CBC journalists had taken a run at Stephen Harper because they disagreed with his policies. In the summer of 2006, less than a year after winning his first minority government, CBC used the Israeli-Lebanese war as an excuse to portray Harper as a cold-hearted monster who didn't care about civilians, including children, dying. Reporter Christina Lawand took a comment Harper made about polling trends and made it sound like he was rebuking protesters concerned about bloodshed.

The report from the Conservative Party's summer caucus meeting in Cornwall, Ontario showcased a comment from protester Elsaadi Daad, a Muslim woman speaking broken English and wearing the traditional hijab. "And burning children and killing innocent people. I don't care, each side, that's wrong and this has to stop," Ms Daad said to the camera.

Lawand then narrated a bridge between Daad's statement and the Prime Minister's. "And while Elsaadi Daad was invited to deliver her message directly to Canada's foreign affairs minister, Stephen Harper clearly wasn't swayed," Lawand said, immediately before playing a clip of Harper.

"I'm not concerned or preoccupied in any way with reaction within individual communities. I think that reaction is entirely predictable," Harper was quoted as saying.

While the quote was entirely accurate, the context was not.

Lawand had made it seem as if Harper was addressing

the concerns of the protesters with his comment about not being concerned. In fact he was responding to a question on polling and claims that the Conservatives were gaining the support of Jewish voters and losing support among Muslim voters over his stand on Israel.

Harper was actually asked about his views on the protesters outside his meeting and about what he had said to Ms. Daad, but CBC chose not to use that clip. What Harper did say was that his ministers regularly communicate with communities that have strong views on the issue. "We have a responsibility as a government to understand all perspectives," Harper said. He went on to say that many groups had strongly held views. "They can't and shouldn't be ignored and can't and shouldn't guide all of our decisions at the same time."

Harper's comments were vastly different from what CBC had reported, but taking comments on one issue and using them completely out of context fit the agenda of making the Conservatives seem cold and uncaring. CBC would offer an apology more than two weeks later, a brief statement at the end of the newscast just before signing off, a much weaker placement to report their error than they had given the biased piece in the first place.

While governments have been complaining about journalists and their coverage since the two groups first met, some reports are so bad that a formal complaint must be made. That's what happened with a CBC *National* report on government anti-smoking initiatives in early December 2010.

Reporter Diana Swain reported that government plans to expand the graphic warning labels on cigarette packages had been "shelved" due to meetings with lobbyists from big tobacco. During a four minute, story

155

Swain asserted that the reason for the government shelving their plans "seems to be a sophisticated lobby effort working behind the scenes and coordinated by tobacco companies on all kinds of topics."

Swain drew a direct link between that lobbying effort and the government not meeting a previously announced timeline for unveiling a new anti-smoking strategy. Airtime was given to Physicians for a Smoke-Free Canada and to, Manitoba's NDP health minister but not to the government point of view. A press officer had provided Swain and producers at CBC with written statements on the matter, as had the Prime Minister's office, but none of the statements were included in the original story. Instead CBC simply said that Health Minister Leona Aglukkaq was not available, giving the impression she just might be hiding.

Dimitri Soudas, the director of communications for the Prime Minister filed a formal complaint. In a letter to CBC's Ombudsman, Soudas wrote that he had concerns with "both the process by which the story was put together and the factual content of the story itself."

Soudas pointed out that producers for the segment had told a contact in the Prime Minister's press office that CBC was looking for details on seven different meetings between lobbyists and a policy advisor for the Prime Minister. The PMO was not clearly told that the story was on the issue of cigarette warning labels, which may have aided in CBC getting a quicker response. No deadline was given for the report, just that the airdate was not "imminent." When the press officer called back four days later to say they were still working on the request, the PMO was informed that CBC was airing the report that night. There simply was no time left to respond.

Soudas went on to complain that Swain had asked for an interview and been turned down, but "nevertheless flew to Ottawa and filmed herself grandstanding in the House of Commons foyer for her report." Aglukkaq's office had provided two written responses to CBC, neither of which made the report.

A CBC viewer would have been forgiven for thinking that big tobacco was barking and the government was jumping. That, however, wasn't the case.

Part of the written response on why the new anti-smoking plans were delayed included comments explaining that the government was planning to use social media strategies as a way to reach young people. A couple of months later, when the government plan was unveiled, that very strategy was highlighted.

It would also be revealed that the thrust of the meetings between the government and tobacco lobbyists had been the illegal tobacco trade, the kind not subject to health inspection, warning labels or any government control. Contraband tobacco was a growing problem at the time and new warning labels on legitimate cigarettes wouldn't help if the trade in illegal smokes continued to grow.

CBC Ombudsman Kirk Lapointe reviewed the formal complaint from Soudas, and while he mused about whether the Prime Minister's office should even be allowed to complain given their influence over CBC's budget, he eventually did side with the government. Lapointe said that the story and the conclusions reached were, "insufficiently supported to meet CBC's Journalistic Standards and Practices that call for facts and evidence to arrive at conclusions."

Canadian conservatives are not the only ones CBC likes to target. The state broadcaster loves attacking foreign conservatives as well.

In the 2008 US presidential campaign, Republican vice-presidential nominee Sarah Palin was a favourite target of criticism at CBC. It mattered not that she could draw crowds bigger than John McCain, that she was a successful mother, politician and wife – that she seemed to have it all. For CBC, that Palin was a conservative was enough reason to knock her down.

In early September 2008, just days after McCain announced that Palin would be his running mate on the Republican ticket, CBC commentator Heather Mallick let loose with a column that reverberated on both sides of the border:

> "I assume John McCain chose Sarah Palin as his vice-presidential partner in a fit of pique because the Republican money men refused to let him have the stuffed male shirt he really wanted. She added nothing to the ticket that the Republicans didn't already have sewn up, the white trash vote, the demographic that sullies America's name inside and outside its borders yet has such a curious appeal for the right.

> "So why do it?

> "It's possible that Republican men, sexual inadequates that they are, really believe that women will vote for a woman just because she's a woman."

And that was Mallick just getting warmed up. She went on:

> "Palin has a toned-down version of the porn actress look favoured by this decade's woman,

the over treated hair, puffy lips and permanently alarmed expression."

CBC received more than 300 complaints about the piece after it was reported on by media outlets on both sides of the border. Then ombudsman for the state broadcaster, Vince Carlin, wrote that while Mallick was free to express her opinions her writing should still meet CBC's standards:

"Policy calls for opinions to be based on fact. Ms. Mallick's item generally stays in the opinion column but she does offer some flat statements that appear to offer "facts" without any backup. For instance, there is no factual basis for a broad scale conclusion about the sexual adequacy of Republican men. In fact, that type of comment, applied to any other group, would easily be seen as, at best, puerile. Similarly, the characterization of Palin supporters as white trash lacks a factual basis."

Carlin took CBC editors to task for not vetting Mallick's piece properly, and then he did something shocking. He admitted the left wing bias of CBC:

"On CBCNews.ca, there does not appear to be a wide range of "pointy" views. For instance, many of those who complained claimed that there is no one of an opposite ideological viewpoint readily apparent on the service. Unfortunately, this appears to be true."

18

CBC's Bought And Paid For Media Cronies

How does CBC get away with all of their shenanigans? How can the state broadcaster vilify respected doctors and business leaders, leading to multi-million dollar lawsuits and settlements all paid for by you? How can CBC refuse to release the same kind of information that every other government department or agency releases? How can they use tax dollars to attack their enemies?

And ultimately, how can CBC do all of this without generating serious media criticism?

The answer is simple: CBC makes sure that it is not in the financial interests of other media outlets and key reporters to ever say anything negative about the state broadcaster.

It is true that outside of Sun Media there is some criticism of CBC, but that is mostly confined to the arts pages with complaints of CBC not putting enough ballet on the air.

But political coverage of CBC is almost non-existent and, where it appears, exclusively positive. CBC is able to achieve this remarkable feat through a series of agreements, some of them involving money paid to journalists.

A 2001 agreement between CBC's French services and Montreal's French language broadsheet *La Presse* saw both parties agree to work on joint stories and offer cross promotion of each other's properties. It also spoke of plans to work on joint commercialization of web sites. It doesn't take a genius to realize that a newspaper that has joined with the state broadcaster to produce joint stories, and work commercially together, will be unwilling to write critically of their new partner.

The agreement, signed by CBC's then vice-president of French services Sylvain Lafrance, and Guy Crevier the president and editor of *LaPresse*, was given an unlimited time line. It helps explain articles and columns, such as those by Vincent Marissal, that give CBC a pass on so much.

LaPresse isn't the only major newspaper with a deal that gives them access to CBC material while appearing to come with a muzzle for the paper's journalists.

At one time *The National Post* ran a regular feature called CBC Watch which pointed out the left wing bias of the state broadcaster as well as errors in their over-heated, anti-American, anti-conservative and anti-Israel stories. That regular feature eventually faded into the background, and after October 2009, criticism of CBC in the pages of the *Post* virtually dried up.

On October 1, 2009, CBC and the *Post* issued a statement announcing their new partnership. "CBC.ca will run daily financial stories and podcasts from the *Financial Post* in CBC's online Money section, and *The National Post* will run daily sports stories in the sports section of nationalpost.com and periodically in the sports section of the newspaper. Financial terms were not disclosed."

Executives from both companies were effusive about the deal.

"This partnership builds on key strengths of two great news organizations," Paul Godfrey, president and CEO of *National Post* said in the statement. "For more than a century, the *Financial Post* has been Canada's go-to brand for business and the CBC is a leader in sports coverage. Together, we will provide Canadians the best in business and sports news."

CBC's Richard Stursberg called the deal, "an attractive arrangement for both organizations."

"As Canada's national public broadcaster, we have an unsurpassed reputation in the field of sports reporting, which will be available to more Canadians through the *Post*'s readership. CBC.ca's financial news content will be enhanced by one of Canada's most trusted and respected sources of business news," Stursberg said.

It was a wise move on the part of Stursberg. He gained respected business content for CBC, an organization which even he called anti-business, while also silencing a harsh critic. The *Post* was, and still is, struggling financially and couldn't turn down the offer of free stuff in exchange for changing their tune on CBC.

And boy did the *Post* change its tune.

In April 2012 as the news of CBC's rather mild budget cuts was still being talked about, Jonathan Kay, the man who had started up CBC Watch, wrote a column for the *Post* calling for CBC to be a well-funded public broadcaster.

Kay wrote that commercial radio, for the most part, was not worth listening to: "It's wrong to say that all of it caters to the lowest common denominator. But most of it does." He then said that while some might find the cost of CBC too high, we really shouldn't if we want to be part of the civilized world.

"Do we want to become the only nation in the OECD without a substantial public broadcaster? Putting ads on Radio One would take us down that road. That prospect might not mean much to Canadians who get their news exclusively from the web or newspapers, or who want nothing from their talking boxes except sex and screaming and incontinence jokes. But for the rest of us, it seems like a bad bargain: A thousandth of our GDP is not too high a price to spend for a smarter Canada."

"But for the rest of us, it seems like a bad bargain: A thousandth of our GDP is not too high a price to spend for a smarter Canada."

From harsh critic to calling CBC the key to a smarter Canada! Fascinating! Of course this was also Kay's way of saying he wants the rest of us to subsidize his news and entertainment choices by calling for a commercial free CBC while he works in the lowly world of advertiser and subscriber supported media.

While other news outlets don't have direct agreements with, CBC that doesn't mean they don't have a vested interest in keeping CBC happy.

Canadian Press used to be the dominant news wire service in Canada. Everyone belonged to CP and everyone shared content and covered expenses. CP set the national agenda in Canada - It used to. While smaller than it used to be, CP is still a force to be reckoned with, especially when it comes to Parliamentary coverage.

The state broadcaster has long been one of the biggest, if not the very largest, customer of Canadian Press. CP doesn't do negative stories about CBC executives living large on the taxpayer dime. Cabinet Minister Bev Oda can travel in a limo and bill taxpayers for a $16 orange juice while on a trip to Britain and it is huge news for days. CBC executives travelling 30 minutes from their offices to occupy a resort and spend $1,400 on booze! That's not a story!

Writing stories critical of your biggest customer would be bad for business and CP knows it.

In the fall of 2011, as the court battle between CBC and Information Commissioner Suzanne Legault was heating up, CP covered the story, but mainly as a way to defend CBC and attack Sun Media for daring to ask how tax dollars were being spent. Remarkably the reporter that CP assigned to cover the story was already on the CBC payroll.

When a reporter from another media outlet appears on CBC they get paid for their time. The payment scale varies but for political shows such as CBC's *Power and Politics,* the fee is generally about $250 per appearance. For The *National*'s At Issue Panel, the fee is $500 plus travel and hotel expenses. Jennifer Ditchburn appeared on both shows on a regular basis all while covering CBC for The Canadian Press.

When blogger and conservative activist Dean Skoreyko filed a complaint with CP's editor in chief, it was dismissed. "I would have concern about conflict if Ms. Ditchburn was on contract with CBC and it was a significant part of her income," White wrote in response.

At the time, Ditchburn was appearing once or twice a week on *Power and Politics* and was a regular fill-in on the At Issue Panel. That means that she was earning $1,000-$2,000 per month from *Power and Politics* plus her money and paid for trips to Toronto which added $500 per appearance.

To some people that amount of money isn't a lot, but for others, it is equal to their monthly income. How many seniors in this country live on less? Yet to CP this was a modest amount of money. White also dismissed the complaint by saying that Ditchburn wasn't on contract with CBC, yet documents obtained under access to information showed that the state broadcaster considered Ditchburn an employee with her own employee number.

Other documents showed that Ditchburn, due to her position and positive coverage of CBC, was being offered exclusive access to Hubert Lacroix and internal CBC documents.

Ditchburn isn't alone among journalists appearing on CBC for money. For many journalists covering Ottawa and the comings and goings of the federal government, getting a coveted spot on CBC as a guest panelist is a dream come true. Speaking ill of Mother Corp, as they call it would not help in landing one of those spots.

While CP played CBC cheerleader, its owners also kept silent. Since 2010 CP has been owned by three major newspaper companies – *The Globe and Mail*, *The Toronto Star* and Gesca, the owner of *LaPresse*.

LaPresse already had an agreement with CBC prior to buying CP but now, along with *The Globe* and *The Star*, they had newfound reasons not to write critically of the state broadcaster – it could annoy a major customer. *LaPresse* has rarely ever been critical of the CBC, and readers of *The Globe* are what Richard Stursberg called the CBC's constituency, so criticism of the state broadcaster wouldn't make sense. As for *The Star*, the most left-wing newspaper in Canada, it restricts its critique of CBC to complaints that its programs might be appealing to the wrong kinds of people, or that they let someone air a conservative viewpoint on the news. Beyond that, *The Star* is willing to let CBC continue to attack the successful, issue huge payouts in lawsuits and spend tax dollars frivolously. After all, at the end of the day, CBC is just as left-wing as *The Star* – and that's what matters.

Not surprisingly, CBC stories exposing problems with the state broadcaster come from one source, Sun Media.

19

What To Do Now

By now you've learned that CBC is a media outlet out of control. Despite all their claims that they are accountable to Parliament and to the people of Canada, the attitude at the top remains that CBC is accountable to no one.

This is an organization that continues to destroy lives and reputations without regard for those they hurt. The only reason they can continue to do so is because they know they have bags of money to pay for lawyers. If CBC were like most media outlets and required to earn their keep such lawsuits would not be tolerated.

Neither would the waste at CBC.

Each year CBC spends more than $1 billion taxpayer dollars and it refuses to say how a large portion of that money is spent. How big is Hubert Lacroix's bonus? Was he the one given a bonus of $165,090 or 3.5 times the average Canadian income? We'll never know.

How much money from the annual taxpayer subsidy does CBC hand over to NHL President Gary Bettman? The state broadcaster uses its deep, taxpayer-filled pockets to outbid every private sector broadcaster for the rights but refuses to release costs.

The answer to all of these problems of course is to privatize CBC and take it off the public dole. Would you care how much a privately owned CBC paid for the rights to *Hockey Night in Canada*? Would you care what the CBC president took home for a bonus if you weren't paying for the bonus?

And, as for defending frivolous lawsuits that could be settled with an apology, that wouldn't matter either if CBC were in private hands.

This isn't a new proposition. It has been floated before, even by a Liberal cabinet minister. In 2004, then Revenue Minister Stan Keyes was caught on mic airing his real views about CBC - while on a CBC show of all places. During a break in taping, Keyes said, CBC "has become a monster, quite frankly."

"It's a billion dollars we have put towards CBC television and we witness direct competition between a public broadcaster and the private sector," Keyes said.

Nothing came of the idea of selling CBC back then, but that doesn't mean the possibility is dead.

While the Harper government is loath to inflict any real damage on the CBC budget for fear of angering all the right people, a serious private sector bid to buy CBC would have to be considered.

What would such a bid look like?

Imagine for a moment an existing broadcaster, one with limited exposure in English television, teaming up with a major pension fund - and to make the deal politically correct, one or more of the aboriginal investment funds that exists. Such a bid, for the English only assets of CBC would have to be taken seriously.

A similar proposal for the French language assets could be made.

Until such a bid becomes a reality, there is still something you can do to push CBC towards privatization. Fight for the hearts and minds of your friends, family and neighbours. Many of the people you know likely don't think very much about CBC, mostly because outside of hockey, they don't watch it.

By convincing those around you, including elected officials, that selling off CBC is a good thing for Canada, you can help change the conversation about the state broadcaster.

Here's how.

What you can do?

Lobbying your Member of Parliament

When many Canadians get upset about an issue they fire off an email to the Prime Minister. While that is an important step in making sure the government of the day hears your voice, it is not the only step. The first step should be contacting your local MP.

In reality it doesn't matter if your MP is a fan of the CBC or wishes they had never existed, making sure that your MP knows how you feel should be the first step. No government will attempt any change if they do not think that the local MPs will support it. Lobby campaigns in favour of CBC are very effective and those who want change in the other direction must be equally effective.

Some MPs are already onside with the idea of selling off CBC, but they need to know that you have their back. While some like Calgary MP Rob Anders can be outspoken, others are fearful of a backlash, and might get cold feet if there are too many complaints that any changes at CBC will result in lost jobs or the local pet grooming show being cancelled. Tell you MP loud and clear that you want the CBC sold off and that you will support them in their efforts.

Know your MP's office

Each MP has at least one office in their riding and one on Parliament Hill. Find out if there is a specific staff member who deals with policy questions for your member of Parliament, or if there is someone designated to liaising with the public. Make sure you get to know that person and ensure that they are aware of your feelings about CBC.

Every Canadian is able to contact their own MP by mail free of charge using Canada Post. The address for all MPs is the same.

(NAME OF YOUR MP)
House of Commons
Parliament Buildings
Ottawa, Ontario
K1A 0A6

If you use this format, there is no need to put a stamp on the outside of the envelope.

As you write your letter, keep your points brief, but include a couple of facts that support your argument.

Are you most upset about CBC's bias? Take an example from earlier in this book to back up the claim or find a more recent example from today's news reports. If you are bothered by the lawsuits and reputations ruined, mention a few of the cases and ask your Member of Parliament if they are familiar with the cases. Chances are they have never heard of them.

Make sure that you let your MP know that you actually live in their constituency and will be casting your ballot in the next election. Letters should be brief and to the point and always polite. Use a spellchecker before sending it off.

Snail mail may seem like an antiquated way to contact an MP, but given the number of emails each and every office gets, an old fashioned letter is likely to stand out.

Email

Email is an instantaneous method of communication which can be both a blessing and a curse. If you read this book and then run for the computer to fire off an email, take a moment and pause to ask yourself a few questions.

Does this email sound like it comes from a sane, rational person who an MP would be happy to meet in public, or an angry person who might have security called on them? Being angry won't win the argument.

Have I kept my points brief (under one page printed) and backed them up with facts? Supporting your arguments with facts could change the mind of an MP who is on the fence, or give backbone to those who already agree with you.

Have I checked the spelling of my letter, including the MP's name? This may seem like a small and obvious point, but firing off an angry quick email will likely result in mistakes which can lessen the impact of your argument.

Once you have done all this make sure that you have the email of your MP correct, then consider adding in the email address of the Prime Minister.

The prime minister's email address is pm@pm.gc.ca

You can find your MP's email address by searching for you MP by postal code at http://parl.gc.ca

Presenting a petition

Whether your Member of Parliament agrees or disagrees with your cause, they are obligated by convention to present your petition to the House of Commons. Every citizen of Canada is free to petition Parliament on an issue - but there are guidelines. Follow these guidelines, collect the names and signatures of your friends, family members, club members or like-minded individuals, and then present the final document to your MP. They will then present it to the House of Commons where it will be put into the public record.

Lobby the Prime Minister

While the most important person to contact in a lobbying campaign for changes at CBC is your local MP, contacting the office of the Prime Minister is also important. While the PMO, as it is called, will not deal directly with your complaint or request about CBC, they do keep track of correspondence and forward letters and emails on to the appropriate departments.

The Prime Minister is also briefed on what issues

Canadians are contacting his office about, and how many contacts the office receives on a particular issue.

If you write to the Prime Minister about CBC, you are likely to receive a form letter or email in reply, telling you that your concerns have been shared with the Minister of Heritage. Do not despair. Passing your communication, be it letter or email, on to the respective Minister in charge of the file is standard protocol. By sending your concerns through the Prime Minister's office, you ensure that your comments have been noticed by the highest office in the land, and that the minister in charge is hearing about the issue from his boss.

Lobbying your neighbours

Equally important as lobbying politicians is sharing what you have learned with your circle of influence. Each of us is in contact with family, friends or neighbours who share our point of view on issues. Have you shared what you have learned about CBC with your friends?

Maybe your friends feel generally the same way about CBC as you do, but have never really given the state broadcaster much thought. Now is the time to activate them. Share the stories from this book with them. Tell them how they can help you make changes. Have them sign your petition or write to their MP.

Social media

Canadians love social media, especially Facebook. While Twitter, Pinterest and other sites have grown in popularity, Facebook remains the dominant form of social media in Canada. Use this free service to spread the word about CBC. If you see a story highlighting their waste of tax dollars or their secrecy share it. If you see an example of obvious bias, point it out to your Facebook friends.

In every instance, encourage them to share your postings with their friends. Each of those friends also has their own networks. Once an item is shared, it can take on a life of its own and help expose the truth about CBC to a much wider audience.

Letters to the Editor

Here is another seemingly old fashioned method of airing your views in public to a dedicated audience. Every day, thousands of people look to the letters section of their papers first. Follow the same format as other communications. Be brief and calm, and present facts to back up your claims. Use any instance of CBC making the news to get your point across that CBC must be sold.

Call talk radio

Each day millions of Canadian listens in to the exchange of ideas on talk radio. Many stations have open line; open topic segments during the day, or a host may actually be soliciting views on the state broadcaster due to a news story that day. Whatever the opportunity make your voice heard – call in!

Participate in town halls or public consultations

Whether they are held by individual MPs, Parliamentary committees or regulators like the Canadian Radio-television Telecommunications Commission, there is no shortage of public meetings on any given topic. Often though only one side appears and only one side has their point of view heard, especially on issues such as the CBC. Lovers of the state broadcaster are well organized and well-funded. They make sure that, when MPs look for input from the public, their point of view is heard loud and clear.

Up until now, most opponents of CBC have just reacted to the state broadcaster with indifference, at best, simply giving the organization a shrug. Armed with the right facts you can make sure not only that your voice is heard, but that it has impact.

If appearing at a public meeting, find out ahead of time if you must register to speak. If so, register as early as possible and encourage as many of your friends to do the same. Some public meetings do not require registration to speak and will simply take comments from the floor. If that is the type of meeting you are attending, arrive early and make sure that you and your group are strategically placed. Split up if need be, so that someone from your group is seated near every microphone that may take questions or statements from the floor.

Prepare your questions ahead of time. If your question is rambling and touches on many points, it is easier for a politician or bureaucrat to side step your main concern by speaking about something else you raised. If your question if short and to the point, it is much more difficult to evade it. If the public meeting is about CBC funding, then split up the questions. Have one person ask why there should be any funding at all, while someone else asks what Parliament could do with an extra billion dollars per year. That's about $100 million dollars every 30 days, money better used for health care, education, defence.

Some forms of public consultation will not actually allow the public to speak, but will take written submissions. Make sure you find out what format written submissions must take. Are there word limits? Do you need to fill out specific forms, or will a couple of type-written pages suffice? Complete your submission a couple of days before the deadline and have a friend you trust go over your submission ahead of time to make sure you have made your points clearly and concisely.

A growing trend is for MPs to use electronic town halls either by telephone or website. The same rules apply. Find out if you need to register and follow any rules laid out. Come armed with friends and facts. While being a lone wolf and arguing with those you oppose in an online session can be fun, having back-up can take some of the pressure off and change the mood from an e-lynching to a reasoned discussion.

Follow up, follow up, follow up

Once you have engaged your Member of Parliament, look for follow up opportunities. Don't assume that one letter or email will change their mind. Remind them of your concerns at public meetings, community BBQs or with a short but polite phone call to their office.

The job of convincing the government to sell CBC will not be an easy one, but it can be done with your help and your hard work. Act now! YOU can make a difference!

Appendix

Presenting a petition to your MP

The House of Commons website offers advice for how to properly present a petition. You can find the guidelines at this link and reprinted below.

http://www.parl.gc.ca/About/House/PracticalGuides/ Petitions/petitionsPG2008__Pg02-e.htm

Introduction

Before a petition can be presented by a Member, it must be examined to confirm that it meets certain requirements established by the rules and practices of the House (described below). A Member wishing to present a petition must first submit the petition to the Clerk of Petitions for certification.

Form of a Petition

Addressee
A petition must be addressed to one of the following:
the House of Commons;
the House of Commons in Parliament assembled;
the Government of Canada;
a Minister of the Crown; or
a Member of the House of Commons.

Text

A petition must contain a request, sometimes also referred to as a prayer, for the addressee to take some action (or refrain from taking some action) to remedy a grievance.

A petition may also include a more detailed description of the grievance and/or a statement of opinion. However, a statement of grievance or opinion alone cannot be received as a petition.

The request should be clear and to the point.

The petition must not demand or insist that the addressee do something.

The petition may include a return address.

Written, Typewritten or Printed on Paper of Usual Size

The text of a petition must be handwritten, typed, printed or photocopied on sheets of paper of usual size, i.e. measuring 21.5 cm x 28 cm (8 ½ x 11 inches) or 21.5 cm x 35.5 cm (8 ½ x 14 inches). A petition submitted on paper of irregular size, or on any other material, is not acceptable.

Language

A petition must be respectful, use temperate language, and not contain improper, disrespectful or unparliamentary language. In particular, there should be no disrespect shown to the Sovereign or charge made against the character or conduct of Parliament, the courts or any other duly constituted authority.

A petition must be written in one or both of the official languages.

Erasures or Interlineations

The text of a petition must not be altered either by erasing or crossing out words or by adding words or commentary. Any alteration will make the petition unacceptable.

Attachments, Appendices or Extraneous Material

A petition must be free of any other matter attached or appended to or written or printed on the petition, whether in the form of additional documents, maps, pictures, logos, news articles, explanatory or supporting statements, or requests for support. A petition printed on the reverse of a document (for example a newsletter or a Member's Householder or Ten Percenter) is not acceptable.

Subject-Matter Indicated on Every Sheet

If a petition is composed of more than one sheet of signatures and addresses, the subject-matter of the petition must be indicated on every sheet.

Content

Matters Within Federal Jurisdiction

A petition must concern a subject within the authority of the Parliament of Canada, the House of Commons or the Government of Canada. A petition must not concern a purely provincial or municipal matter or any matter which should be brought before a court of law or a tribunal.

Requesting Expenditure of Public Funds

A petition may include a request for the expenditure of public funds.

Signatures and Addresses

A petition must contain a minimum of 25 valid signatures with addresses.

A petition should contain signatures of residents of Canada only. Persons not resident in Canada cannot petition the House of Commons of Canada. A petition signed exclusively by non-resident persons is not acceptable.

There is no minimum age requirement for anyone signing a petition.

Each petitioner must sign, not print, his or her own name directly on the petition and must not sign for anyone else. If a petitioner cannot sign because of illness or a disability, this must be noted on the petition and the note signed by a witness.

A petition must contain original signatures written directly on the document and not pasted, taped, photocopied or otherwise transferred to it.

Some signatures and addresses must appear on the first sheet with the text of the petition. Signatures and addresses may appear on the reverse of the petition.

The address may either be the petitioner's full home address, or the city and province, or the province and postal code. As with the signature, the address must be written directly on the document and not pasted, taped, photocopied or otherwise transferred to it. The inclusion of other contact information (such as telephone numbers or email addresses) is permitted but not required.

A Member of the House of Commons may sign a petition, but should ask another Member to present that petition. The signatures of Members inscribed on a petition are not counted towards the required 25 signatures and addresses.

Draft Petitions

Members of the public who wish to petition the House of Commons on a matter of public interest are advised to first submit a draft petition (without signatures) to a Member of Parliament to see whether it is correctly worded and whether the Member would agree to present it.

(Endnotes)

i.   CBC v Leenen para 175

ii.   The *Globe and Mail* Sat Jul 28 2001 Page: R1

iii. CMAJ June 13, 2000 vol. 162 no. 12 retrieved April 16, 2012
      – http://www.cmaj.ca/content/162/12/1735

iv.   CMAJ June 13, 2000 vol. 162 no. 12 retrieved April 16, 2012
      – http://www.cmaj.ca/content/162/12/1735

v.   CMAJ June 13, 2000 vol. 162 no. 12 retrieved April 16, 2012
      – http://www.cmaj.ca/content/162/12/1735

vi.   CMAJ June 13, 2000 vol. 162 no. 12 retrieved April 16, 2012
      – http://www.cmaj.ca/content/162/12/1735

vii. CBC v Leenen para 198

viii. Ibid para 181

ix.   CBC v Leenen para 175

x.   *Globe and Mail*, December 21, 2007

xi.   *The Hill Times*, May 3, 2010, http://www.hilltimes.com/the-q-a-by-kate-malloy/2010/05/03/q%2526ampa-with-harvey-cashore-truth-shows-up-on-airbus-scandal-but-canada/23764?page_requested=4)

xii. http://www.amazon.ca/On-The-Take-Corruption-Mulroney/dp/0770427081/ref=sr_1_4?s=books&ie=UTF8&qid=1332817166&sr=1-4

xiii. *A Secret Trial*: Brian Mulroney, Stevie Cameron and the Public Trust. William Kaplan page 71

xiv. *National Post*,Fri Oct 1 2010 Page: PM11

xv.   http://www.parl.gc.ca/HousePublications/Publication.aspx?Language=E&Mode=1&Parl=39&Ses=2&DocId=3093030#OOB-2186711

xvi. http://www.parl.gc.ca/HousePublications/Publication.aspx?DocId=3212380&Language=E&Mode=1&Parl=39&Ses=2

xvii. CBC.ca, February 13, 2008

xviii. *The Hill Times,* May 3, 2010, http://www.hilltimes.com/the-q-a-by-kate-malloy/2010/05/03/q%2526ampa-with-harvey-cashore-truth-shows-up-on-airbus-scandal-but-canada/23764?page_requested=3

xix. *Toronto Sun,* Sunday, August 08, 2010 http://www.torontosun.com/news/canada/2010/08/08/14962161.html

xx. ibid

xxi. *The Tower of Babble: Sins, Secrets and Successes Inside the CBC,* Stursberg 2012 page 14

xxii. *The Tower of Babble:* page 17

xxiii. *The Tower of Babble:* page 16

xxiv. http://www.cmf-fmc.ca/documents/files/archives/env-admin/EnvelopeAllocations_2006-2007.pdf

xxv. *The Tower of Babble:* page 96

D

CPSIA information can be obtained at www.ICGtesting.com
Printed in the USA
LVOW081842150213

320347LV00001B/256/P